In 2002 the Find Me ⟨
missing children worldw~~~. ~~~ ~~~~~~~
almost immediately to locate all missing persons.
Missing person investigations are very difficult to solve, mainly because if no evidence or clues are left for investigators then no one knows if the missing person went north, south, east or west. I decided at that time to investigate if the psychic phenomenon was real or false and to determine if their information could be utilized to locate these missing individuals. Since I had never met a psychic I made inquiries and located a psychic in Arizona. From that moment on I interviewed thousands of psychics from all around the world and eventually set up a vetting system that would identify gifted psychics. I also created training systems that would enhance the abilities of those that were struggling in perfecting their gift.

During the building process certain well known psychics in the business provided names of other well known gifted psychics and Jeanette Healey's name was immediately brought to my attention. Jeanette joined the Find Me Group in 2003 and has been a loyal and trusted member since that time. Her dedication, trustworthiness and accuracy are exceptional and we have been fortunate to have her as a long-standing member. I am grateful for her abilities, her honesty and her personal fortitude, which are characteristic of her nature.

J.E. "Kelly" Snyder, Founder/CEO The Find Me Group Inc.

Although Jeanette and I have not met in person - there's that Big Pond thing between us - I consider her a dear friend and valued advisor. I have always found her insights and perspective valuable, heart warming and, just at the right moment, humorous. We have worked many missing person cases together for Find Me all over the world, so we have been together through emotional hell and back. Out here where the Apaches and Pima still roam, Jeanette is what we call a straight arrow - trusted, valued and honored.

Dan Baldwin, Writer

Over the many years I have known her Jeanette Healey has been dedicated to the simple principles of truth and compassion. As a member of the organization FIND ME, and featured in the book with the same name, Jeanette selflessly spent endless hours in the search for answers about missing family members. As one of the hyper-sensitive individuals working on investigations Jeanette was able to aid in urgent situations by unconventional means. Her compassionate nature coupled with determination to find the truth of any given scenario is a winning combination for sure!
When I first read her manuscript *The Right Side of the Moon*, I couldn't put it down. Jeanette's style of writing swept me from one scene to another with grace and intrigue.

Victoria Richards, Publicist

The Right Side of The Moon

Jeanette Ann Healey

Copyright © 2016 JEANETTE ANN HEALEY
All rights reserved.
ISBN: 1533638276
ISBN-13: 978-1533638274

DEDICATION

This is dedicated to my dearest little Nan, Gertrude Ann Wilder. Although not my mother, she was my true Mum whom I loved so very much. I have thought of her every day since she left me: of the fun and laughter that we shared and the guidance that she brought into my life. Without her I would have shrivelled inside and faded like a lost soul.

It is also dedicated to my dear John Playford: my stepfather, whom I loved and called Daddy Long Legs. Thank you for helping make difficult moments with my Mum seem better. You made me laugh and you loved me. You were simply the best.

Most of all, it is dedicated to my husband who forgives my oddness because of the true love that we have for one another.

CONTENTS

Acknowledgments

Preface	*How my gift affected my life: the right side of the moon*	1
1	*A knowing about my Spiritual guide Jack: to share how we are together*	3
2	*My early childhood: Oh Lord*	9
3	*The New Inn pub: family present and past*	16
4	*The New Inn pub: its history and some unusual residents*	23
5	*The New Inn pub: inside but far away*	30
6	*Mothers and daughters: a very sensitive child*	34
7	*Family and friends: my teenage years*	40
8	*My dear little Nan: Gertrude Ann Wilder*	57
9	*Becoming a Nurse: the start of the training*	72
10	*Return to Salem's: juggling married life and work*	86
11	*The Residential Home: Kennington Place*	102
12	*My Soul Mate: Marie*	125

13	*Introducing more pals: Elaine and Lynne*	136
14	*Guardian Angels: human and spirit*	144
15	*Back to family: my brother and my Daddy*	155
16	*Jack and the two Jakes*	160
17	*From the outside looking in: using my gift*	166
18	*A famous case: the murders of Lin and Megan Russell*	172
19	*Working for the family: private cases*	177
20	*Dowsing on maps: looking for Danny*	181
21	*Working with other psychics: terrorism and missing persons*	184
22	*A journey into our world: the Soul Searchers*	190
23	*The search for Keith Bennett: unfinished business*	201
24	*Here and now: closing thoughts*	209

ACKNOWLEDGMENTS

I cannot stress enough the importance of family and friends in my life. Without their encouragement I would not have finished my story. A special mention goes to Lara Cavill, Alison Healey and Caroline Bunting for listening and for reading my story, and to my great friends: Victoria Richards and Dan Baldwin from Arizona with their helpful hints that let me pursue my dreams, and Kelly Snyder for his continued support in working with Find Me.

I also want to thank the Police Officers from Ashford, Canterbury, Kent and Merseyside who were opened minded enough to listen and act upon my information.

Finally, I must thank Frances Kirkman for her patience, professionalism and guidance in editing and getting my book published.

PREFACE

How my gift affected my life: the right side of the moon

This is my story. It is the story of what it was like growing up as a psychic and how that gift has influenced my life.

Why did I call my book *The Right Side of the Moon*? I am drawn to the moon, and it has always fascinated me to look up at the moon's eerie shape, to watch the clouds that drift on past it and shield it from our view. Many people are afraid of being outside when it's dark. I am not one of those people; it doesn't frighten me, as long as I can look up at the sky and see the moon. The eclipse of the sun when the dark moon slowly creeps over it in a short dominance is so wonderful. I love the experience of being plunged into darkness and then the thrill of the sun appearing again.

The first time I can recall an eclipse of the sun I was at the Newtown Catholic Junior School. We were all sent outside to the playground to watch it. At first all the children were silent, but as the sun reappeared again whole, the playground was filled with laughter and shouting. The excitement was wonderful. Years ago as a child I would not have used the word 'amazing' but it *was* amazing.

The moon features a lot in my life. I seem to work better at night, under the dark sky and the wonderful stars. Most of my working life has been on night duty as a nurse in hospitals, a residential home and a short period working on the district. Being psychic, I have found the spirits want to talk all night so occasionally one has to shout and swear to make them go away and leave me alone. Of course, it's important not to do this in front of the patients!

But why the right side of the moon? If you are standing and staring up at it and you can think of a clock showing the time, well, I was born on the right side of the clock and hence the right side of the moon.

I was born at 3.20 in the morning. I shot out very quickly: start to finish two hours, "Hello everyone!"

Apparently, a few hours later, I was taken from the Nursery and given to another mother who, naturally, became upset and shouted out, "This not my baby, my baby is fair haired." - I had a mass of black hair. My mother took offence and thought she was saying that I was not as lovely as her baby.

So our distressed relationship had begun.

CHAPTER 1

A knowing about my Spiritual guide Jack: to share how we are together

I was a small child when I first became aware that there was someone around me. I felt a small breeze and a soft murmuring voice in my mind and not in my ears, especially at night. As I grew older I heard footsteps on the stairs in our home at Cryol Road in Ashford, Kent. When I told my Mum she would get cross and tell me off, "Jeanette, stop being so silly and go to sleep."

Then the voice became louder and the voice was clearer. I knew straight away that it was a male voice: the voice of an older man around my Father's age. It has always been a soft voice but now it has more depth to it. He tried always to help me not to do things that would be detrimental to my well being; unfortunately, I did not always listen. I was always too trusting with people and it took me years to change.

I did not see Jack until I was a young adult as he thought he would unnerve me because I was a nervous child that cried easily. Then one day I asked him, "What is your name and who are you?"

Back came the reply, "I am Jack and I have always been with you. I am one of the old Magicians and have lived off the land in the forests of England and Wales eating berries, plants and the wild life." I realised he was a spirit guide sent to help me. This made me feel happy and also very lucky. Over the years, I have wondered why me and if others have protectors. I have never felt fear of him.

After that, I started to see him as well as hear him. At first when he came it was in a vision in my mind; I could only see his head and he wore dark glasses like the ones that the singer Roy Orbison used to wear. I wondered why he did not show me his eyes. His reply was simply, "It's better this way."

When I was in my early twenties I asked him to come as a whole person, and so he did.

I saw a man 5ft 10" in height and of medium build with shoulder length dark hair that had silver streaks in it. He was wearing a dark inky blue robe to the ground. Such a handsome face! But he was still wearing the glasses. A few weeks later, I asked him to please remove them and so he did. What a shock, as he has the most piercing beautiful blue eyes, like sparkling jewels! I realised then that knowing that my eyes do not like the bright sunshine he was wearing the dark glasses so his eyes didn't dazzle mine.

Jack has such a soft voice, and he never gets cross with me. I think he despairs when I am not heeding his advice but sighs and then walks away. It's funny that as

I do sigh such a lot and I always have, most of the time involuntarily. When I was training to become a nurse, a Sister called Ms Cassidy was often heard saying to me in a loud voice, "Stop sighing Nurse!" Even now people say, "That's a loud sigh, whatever is the matter?" I always reply, "Nothing at all."

I am sure it is Jack and me doing it together.

I do sense him around me most of the time and so when I don't, I feel insecure. When I am feeling low and have this notion that my knowing is fading, I ask him to let me know if he is still around me.

One particular time I asked, "Please let me know, where are you, are you still here?"

About twenty minutes later there was an almighty bang. Our daughter had returned to live with us again after finishing University, and we were sitting in the small lounge next to the kitchen in our petite cottage. We both jumped up and went into the kitchen. The light bulb had smashed through the antique white bowl lamp shade that had been held up with three brass chains. Now, both the light bulb and the lamp shade were scattered on the floor in small splintered broken pieces. Lara looked at me and said, "Well, you got your answer then." When my husband returned home from work that evening he said, "Next time, would you ask Jack to let you know in a less expensive way please."

There have been two other people that have seen Jack. One person was a dearest friend, Lynne, who has since passed over. Lynne was a Psychic Artist, and we worked well together over several years in our psychic work. She drew a picture of him but not a very flattering one, with him looking like Jack Nicholson. I see him as more refined. The other person to see him was my eldest lovely grandson Jake, but more about that later.

Sometimes I become aware that someone, perhaps someone whom I have known, perhaps a murdered person, has become stuck and is unable to pass over. If their own relatives or friends do not come forward to take them over, I ask Jack if he will come forward and then take the person with him. Jack has never refused to help. I am shown this as a vision in my mind: Jack with this other spirit beside him, then they fade and go. He has been so gracious over the years in doing this for me and helping so many people.

One such occasion involved a wonderful friend that I made in France: Joy. Living in France gives us the opportunity of meeting lots of new people. We count ourselves extremely lucky that we were introduced to such a lovely couple as Joy and Kevin, who were happily married for 36 years.

Some people turn up in your life for a reason. She and I were in tune psychically. For example, I was ill one day and she and Kevin turned up at our house in the afternoon.

They had been visiting the medieval town Montmorillion when Joy had said, "We have to go and see Jeanette, I sense something is really wrong with her."

Joy was a Sister in a cottage Hospital in England until she retired early to live in France. She was amazing: so clever, a great sense of humour and her naughtiness was really funny.

Sadly, Joy only had a few years here in the France that she loved. One day we were invited over for the day. As we were walking down through the village to their plot of garden - it was separate to their house, as is often the case in towns or villages in France - she asked me if I picked up anything about Kevin. I didn't. What I kept to myself was that I was given information about Joy; I was told that she had cancer. Very soon after, she had it confirmed by her doctor.

Her beloved Kevin did everything a loving husband could have done and was always there for her. They went through all the trauma that having cancer and the treatment brings, staying positive together.

Unfortunately after a period it returned and they had to go back again to England. When we said goodbye we knew that we would not see her again. It was very sad and I cried loads.

Then one night in December 2011 I woke up in the early hours as Joy had come to me.

"I am frightened, Jeanette."

I spoke back, "Please don't be, I will ask my guide to come forward to you and he will look after you. When those on the other side are ready to come for you, they will." I cannot explain why I know this, but this is what I do believe happens, and it just feels comforting to me.

It was like watching a film: my guide Jack appeared in the mist and stood beside him was Joy. They both faded away. The atmosphere in the room seemed calm.

My husband was asleep. I shook him and woke him up to tell him, and also for confirmation of the date and time.

I have shared this because she touched my life, and I want to honour her for who she was and for choosing me to come to when she passed.

Kevin is still a great friend of ours – Bob and he had an instant strong connection like brothers. Joy and I always used to comment on their nonstop chatting and laughing!

CHAPTER 2

My early childhood: Oh Lord

I have always had a quirky brain and see things in a different way. I am a moon person, with the fascination with the dark that that brings. There is something of the darkness that lies within my personality.

When I was a child I found it difficult to go off to sleep early in the summer time and, being a restless type, I would perch on the window sill in my nightie staring out of the window into the dark and look up at the stars. We lived on a Council estate that was surrounded by the countryside and not too far off in the distance you could hear the train, with that all familiar rattling sound that it makes on the tracks, and the toot, toot of the horn. I have always had a good imagination and have been able to visualise many things, travelling on that train to faraway places. I would be standing alone with a small suitcase, waiting with anticipation for it to arrive.

I would say that at heart I am an adventurer and a romantic person. Really, I have quite a conflict within my personality as I am a true home maker, having the Cancer sign.

The adventurer within me gives me a dare-devil side that isn't always apparent to many people when they first meet me. I have always loved balancing on things: for example, climbing out of my bedroom window and walking on the window sill, which was only six inches in width, past the middle fixed window and climbing in through the other large window. It never entered my head that this being on the first floor, some twelve feet above the ground, I could fall and be killed or cripple myself. I had a confidence inside that somehow I would be alright.

When I was about eight I loved the thought of investigating anything and everything. This meant going into places that I shouldn't have gone into, in particular, the main Church of England church in the middle of the town of Ashford. I was told that as a Catholic you should not enter another religious church or you would go to Purgatory and never get into Heaven. I did not believe this as my thoughts were, then and now, God is everywhere! I was a free thinker. Anyway, I would sneak in to look at everything. There were some tiny stairs either side of a long, beautiful stained glass window pane. Being very slight in build, I was able to manipulate my body, twisting and turning, to get to the top of these stairs which led nowhere. The steps were concrete and the space was narrow, but this did not disappoint me as it felt fun doing this, especially with the knowledge that I shouldn't really be doing it. I don't know why they were there or the real function of them, it really did not matter to me. I absolutely love churches and visit as many as possible and always light several candles. I especially enjoy being on my own in them and quite often have a cry over my own thoughts of Jesus on the Cross, and people who have gone physically from me.

Going forward many years, I have found a lovely ancient church here in France just ten minutes away from our hamlet. It is so poor with very little inside it. Here, I have had several experiences of feeling Jesus around me. I have left fresh flowers on the altar, a gift from me of two brass candle sticks that had been my Nan Wilder's and several envelopes full of small change. A year after I started doing this a group of four ladies arrived at my door. The eldest lady had been searching all year to find me. I said I loved doing it, and she smiled and hugged me and speaking in French thanked me. She gave me a large bar of delicious chocolate. What a wonderful thing for me!

Going back in time again, there were many building sites with plenty of houses and a modern church being built in the fifties and sixties. This unusual playground is where I found my skills as a leader, where I had confidence away from Mum, and my imagination excelled. I would gather a few of the local girls and convince them we were going to far off places in the Middle East, especially off to Jericho! One day I hope that I shall go there.

In fact, one of my weird sayings is: *If you keep that up I shall kick you all the way to Jericho.*

How mad is that?

Anyway, back to my story. There we were, a small

group of children with such enthusiasm that we would walk for a quarter of a mile to start climbing mountains of dirt. The dirt was piled high like big sand dunes on this piece of land where they were about to build the new Catholic church, St Simon's. We would be gone all day and then return home dirty but laughing at having had so much fun.

My childhood was full of moments like these. We went to the woods to dig up primroses and violet plants to put in our gardens. Years ago everyone did this as the working class people were short of money. In fact, so many were dug up over the years that they become scarce and in the 1970s it became banned to do this sort of thing. When we were older and could ride our bikes, we would go further afield searching for and picking the bluebells up in the Challock woods and walking around near the lake at the Eastwell Manor house. We were always searching for derelict buildings to go in. The feeling of past has always involved me, rather than future.

It wasn't all fun and games. Within me I have the capacity for loneliness and nostalgia which isn't always a good thing. To pick up on other people's sorrows from such a young age was not really a good talent to have. It leaves traces behind in the soul. Nonetheless, I should and do class myself a fortunate person, since I have also loved and been loved, which is the best thing in the whole wide world.

Childhood brought many things to me, knowing I just wasn't quite the same as my peers. You could say a step out of tune and a sense that sometimes other people were looking through me as if I wasn't really there. I cannot explain it any better, I'm afraid, just not there. I thought of myself as a shy girl and a little odd. But the strange thing is people did and do remember me well from different periods of my life. I never knew until meeting people again in later life that I had made some kind of connection, mostly for being really nice.

I think that perhaps I felt that I wanted to be invisible. Often when visiting relatives' homes I would go off to investigate and hide under beds etc. Very strange I know, and when people started looking for me I would then feel a bit foolish as I always hid for too long and then could not disclose where I was.

My Mum was a cleaner for a posh lady, Mrs Hubbard, and sometimes would be asked to go in on a Saturday, and so I had to go with her and give her a hand with the small jobs. I have a slight OCD which started when tidying the cupboards and lining up the bottles, tins and glasses. One Saturday, when I was about nine or ten, I had a bad tummy and my Mum wouldn't let me use the outside toilet, saying I would make it smell. So several times that morning I could be seen racing down the road into the town to use the Public toilets. I felt beside myself with embarrassment. That is one of the differences between my mother and me: no way would my young child be put in that situation. I would have told Mrs Hubbard that I would be leaving and have taken my child home. She always put strangers before her own. She would feed the dustbin men a cup of soup when it snowed, and what was left over my brother and I were given. All for show, that was her way.

At school I could disappear out of the classroom and nobody would realise that I had gone. My attendance was sporadic in some classes and, for that reason, no one noticed. I just would slip away and rejoin the class again later. Recalling this now I realise just how odd it all was. I did it just to be alone. I had forgotten all of that. Only today has it popped back into my mind. It did not mean that I didn't learn subjects because I did, coming second in the class on more than one occasion. Enjoying and being interested in the subject is the key to it all.

My immediate family consisted of my mother, father and an older brother. We didn't work well together or fit together in many ways, which was a shame. But my brother and I were taught how to speak properly with our elders and to behave ourselves. My parents were good looking people but were ill matched in almost every way possible. My Mum was the extrovert: dogmatic, too bossy, bubbly, full of fun. Her biggest fault was she had to have the last word and was always right. But the fun was always at somebody else's expense, especially mine. Mum had to take charge of all the responsibilities of bringing up the children. Father loved to drink and flirt; unfortunately he was embittered over not being released from his job at the railway works in New Town, where he was working at the time of the war. Not going with his two brothers and friends devastated him. These thoughts took over his way of thinking and determined his behaviour for the rest of his life, which was very sad as we all suffered the consequences. He was a lovely quiet chap but stubborn, not easy to live with. He drove my Mum crazy and pushed the gap between me and her wider. She never got on with her own mother and had a turbulent relationship with three of her four sisters. This resulted in her not liking female company and instead having a preference for male company. That is why my brother was her favourite and that is why I looked to my father as an ally. I miss my Dad very much and try and remember all the good things about him. Mum gave us the best childhood that was possible in her own way. She had a knowing but would deny that she was psychic in any way. The older she got the worse she became with her cruel words towards me, especially in letters that she would write to me and then sign, 'from your loving Mother'.

She made me cry as it all felt so sad. I can sometimes laugh about it now though. Walking on eggshells is the only way I can describe how I felt in her company. My wonderful stepfather, John Playford helped a lot with the difficult moments: he loved me and he made me laugh.

CHAPTER 3

The New Inn pub: family present and past

My brother Ed and I spent most of our summer holidays at Dover in Kent where my Mum's parents were living.

My grandparents managed The New Inn pub in York Street, from before the Second World War until 1962. The pub was renowned for being haunted. Quite a lot of the customers shared odd experiences: the sensation or feeling of being watched time and time again; odd strange smells including women's perfumes, musty smells, and body odour.

Also, quite often people would comment about the air going cold. Certain areas in the pub were more sensitive than other parts, the gentlemen's toilets being one. Then there was a large room that you had to walk through to get to the toilets, the room was used for playing cards or darts and board games. Quite often men would come flying out from the toilets or the large room yelling and swearing, having felt something touch them, or brush past them. The Ladies' toilets were next door, but that area did not seem to be affected. There was a back room, to the right of the main bar, that was used as the family's upper sitting room, but this room did not seem to change in atmosphere and was comfortable.

The area that was the most unpleasant was the pub cellar. We had to pass the entrance to it as the door was on the same level as the family's lower living quarters. As you passed the door there were two steps down into the dining room and then through to a small kitchen with a back door that led to the outside. Sometimes it was very creepy passing by the cellar, and I felt that I could hear voices coming out from in there.

My Nan was well thought of by many people who knew her. She was a hard working woman, but she did have the reputation of being slightly eccentric. Rose, as she was known, rather than Mrs Staveley, ruled that pub with an iron rod. She was always polishing and cleaning. My Grandad was of little help to her, as he suffered with severe bronchial asthma, although he won several cups for bowling, funny that! He was a right old character. He would call the girls, 'you little mares'. "Come here all of you here's some money," he'd say. Usually that was five shillings, which was a lot of money in those days. We took it and ran to the local shop a few doors away and spent it all on sweets. He would demand, "Get lost for the day!" and so we did. He and Nan had a large family but were not really natural parents. The fact was that children appeared to annoy them. The less they saw of you the better was their motto.

Climbing up the Cliffs of Dover, going into the caves and derelict houses, my brother, cousins and I had some wonderful times getting up to mischief. Most of our days were spent playing on the sandy beach and swimming in the sea. Playing hide and seek in the old cemetery that was just up above the alms houses was great fun. It was over the other side of the road and up the street from the pub. When I think of all the danger and scrapes we got into it was incredible that nothing dreadful ever happened.

Although, I did nearly kill my younger cousin Sandra. We were at the top of what is known as the 'zigzag path'. It is just below the main road and above is the magnificent Dover Castle. We had her foot scooter to scoot around on, which was fun. She stood on the front of it, and I stepped on behind her and pushed off with one foot. Before we knew what was happening we were off, hurtling at top speed, two small kids shrieking their heads off. The only way I could stop it was to head for a tree, so I did. To this day I don't know how we survived. Someone must have been watching over us. Cuts, grazes and a buckled scooter, I suppose that wasn't too bad. Although I still got a good hiding from my Mum and a telling off from my Auntie Pam, who sent us off to bed early that night. I had many Aunties but she and my Dad's eldest brother Charlie's wife Myrtle, who was homely, were my favourite Aunties from each side of our families. Auntie Pam was very glamorous and wore beautiful dresses and frequently had cocktail parties. She and my Uncle Les lived in Dover for years and owned a large house which was run as a Bed and

Breakfast. We often stayed with them on a weekend when she and my Mum helped their parents behind the bar serving drinks at busy weekends.

The pub was the width of two small terrace houses, and seemed to stretch endlessly way back. The cellar door was on the same level as the sitting room and kitchen. Outside housed an outside toilet and a walled garden which had a huge rockery garden, plus a resident tortoise that was very large and very old. Terry was his name, yes, it's very original, we go in for simple names for pets. One day Nan had been white-washing everything outside; sometimes poor Terry got in the way and ended up with white splodges on his head and shell. Nan did the scullery as well, "It's clean looking," she said. On the kitchen wall sat this large spider which came out every time I went down there; Nan said it would be unlucky to kill it. It scared me and my cousin Reggie almost to death. I do not like them, and poor old Reggie had had a nasty experience with one in the outside toilet. The cobweb got entangled on his school blazer and in it was a fat black spider. He screamed blue murder, running as fast as he could and rapidly shaking himself but it had stuck like glue. My Dad had to race after him to catch him and detach him from the dreaded thing. Reggie's face was as red as a beetroot and sweaty, what a thing to happen! He refused to go into that toilet again. Of course, we all laughed at his misfortune, as families do.

In many of the old pubs of that time there was a lot of brass and copper. I remember whole strips of brass running up the length of the public bar floor, and the foot rail beneath the bar counter was in copper. The door had brass plates, and on the pumps it seemed everywhere. Nan would give me a duster and I had to follow her rubbing at the brass where she had cleaned it with liquid brass. Nan must have only weighed about six stone, her choice was to smoke and not eat. That was why her hair at the front went yellow in the end. She was an awful cook. I remember that years later when they had retired from the pub, on a Sunday Grandad and I used to argue who was going to try the food first, him or me? The gravy was the worst that I have ever tasted: it was too watery. By contrast my Dad's mother's cooking was lovely: a real treat to eat.

In the middle part of the pub there had been two steps going up to the ground floor area which would lead past the sitting room and on to the darts playing room at the back. As I have mentioned earlier, following on were the gentlemen's toilets. To the left side at the top of the stairs was the telephone cubicle with a seat and a telephone directory hanging from some string tied under the coin box below the phone. Within the framework it had two etched glass windows, one on the side of the boxed telephone and another on the door facing the stairs. I would creep upstairs and try to make myself invisible, hiding in it with a bag of crisps and peering through the clear strips of glass at all the people walking back and forwards with their drinks. It was all very entertaining, but was I actually seeing living people or spirits?

The telephone box was the only place where I did not feel uneasy when I was left alone. I especially had a sense of being watched in the bedroom on the first floor, during the day as well as when I was put to bed at night. The sleeping arrangements meant I slept with my Mum and Dad on the same level as Nan and

Grandad, and my brother, poor sod, had to sleep on his own upstairs in one of the two attic bedrooms. The attic room above our room unnerved me so much that I could never allow myself to venture into it until I was a lot older. I felt too scared of what was up there. So we would call out to each other for reassurance before going to sleep. If my brother had been nasty to me that day I would get my own back by saying THE THING in the next room would get him. He would go mad and rush downstairs and climb in bed with me, until our parents came to bed. They would know that I had said something to frighten him, and he was always reluctant to go to his own bed again. Then Dad had to go up and sleep with him.

One day when I was playing alone in Nan's bedroom looking in her square, chestnut, jewellery box, I happened to look around to find a small boy about my age staring back at me, "Hello, who are you?" I asked. How funny he looked! He was wearing black shiny patent leather shoes with silver buckles. His hair was a beautiful blonde colour with ringlets. I turned away and picked out a small silver necklace to show him, and when I looked back he was gone. "He didn't even say goodbye to me," I said. Later I told my Mum and Nan, "God almighty!" my Mum was yelling, "She's as barmy as my own mother."

Meanwhile, Nan's telling Grandad, "She has seen our little Georgie."

"Don't encourage the girl, Rose, she's got a vivid imagination as it is."

What was going on? That was that, we were packed off home that evening, just put on the train with Mum and Dad back to Ashford and home. Years later Nan told me about Georgie, "Poor little mite, broke his neck falling down the very same flight of stairs from the bedrooms."

As I grew older my Nan sat down with me and said that I had a gift, a knowing, and that not many people had this. She said that she had it, and it was referred to as being a Medium. I could see and hear things that weren't always apparent to others. Unfortunately, Nan did not properly mentor me about it all, and so I kept many things to myself until I was an adult. My Dad had it also but was completely frightened by it and so that wasn't helpful to me either. Having my guide Jack and my own beliefs were my salvation.

CHAPTER 4

The New Inn pub: its history and some unusual residents

The New Inn pub was part of Dover's history. Dover is a historic town that has the magnificent Dover Castle on the cliffs above one of the busiest ports in England. Many ancient Roman discoveries have been found locally. The pub was at 33 York Street, Dover, Kent. Established by the 1850s, it closed in May 1962 and was demolished in December of that year. I feel very sad not to be able to visit it now.

The pub was pulled down, and this helped to destroy a whole community of many terraced houses, small lanes with cobbled paths, that special sweet shop that was on the end of the row that was adjoined to the pub and other shops. The Alms Houses and a working garage were also knocked down to build the dual carriageway. This was to allow the main traffic to get to and from the docks, coming along from the old

Folkestone Road into Dover.

It was a creepy looking pub, four stories high from the basement up to the attic, and looked very deep, from the front to the back. One of the infamous reputations it had, was that it was one of the public houses where in days gone by the local meetings took place of the smugglers, in and around the vast area of the coastland of Kent. There had been a tunnel which connected the New Inn public house with two other old pubs in that area. These two pubs had very odd names. One was called the 'Five Alls' and the other 'Cause is Altered'.

I believe the car park along York Street is where the New Inn pub stood. This is the site where the famous 'Roman Painted House' was discovered in Dover, Kent. The pub cellar and walled garden stood above the site. The designs on the walls of the Painted House are related to Bacchus, the Roman God of wine so it was a fitting site for a pub.

Nan Staveley was a medium and would talk to many spirits there. She was known to speak to a Roman soldier in the cellar. This restless spirit, who was the headless soldier, appeared quite often to her over the years, but never after my grandparents left the pub. They moved to the Buckland estate in Dover, several miles away. Obviously the association was with the land the pub stood on. Don't ask me how she could talk to a spirit with no head, and get a reply! It is a real pity that I do not recall any of their shared conversations.

It has been documented that many people saw a spirit of a Chelsea pensioner in different places in the pub; perhaps they were really seeing a soldier's uniform? I don't recall hearing people speak of it myself but because of my young age I would not have spoken with any customers that visited the pub.

I am so thrilled to think I stayed in that pub as a child. Although certain places like the attic bedroom, the back room, where the customers played darts, and especially the cellar really did frighten and unnerve me. Sometimes it felt as if I could see the rooms through a distorted mirror. As an adult I have seen this many times as a Remote Viewer, especially to do with terrorism. In certain situations, to be able to get into the mind of a person, their entity is shown to me rather than their spirit. Let me try to explain the difference between a spirit and an entity. When a spirit tries to make contact with me it is like looking at a flimsy photo. An entity is very different and is something to be careful about. In my experience, bad people come as entities. An entity has a form that is much heavier than a spirit. It is almost like watching a film. Or perhaps a bubble is more appropriate, with the sense that if you leaned forward and put out your arm or forearm it would go inside that bubble. It is necessary to be very careful with entities.

Nan only allowed me and my brother to go into the cellar if we were with her. I remember her looking at me and saying, "Especially *you* don't go in there on your own."

She warned me, "It would not do you any good to be there on your own." I would say, "Why Nan?" and she would just say, "Off you go now."

I always would hesitate on the steps outside the door, feeling that shiver go down my spine, then I would think better of it and quickly move away. There were many spirits in that pub, and not just the drink kind. I would often feel uneasy. I could not stand the thought of THEM watching us, watching ME. I remember as a young girl the chill in the air as a frightening eeriness, watching and seeing my own breath close in front of me, the sensation of knowing they were there. The spirits knew I could 'Channel', and they only wanted to talk with me. I just wished they would go away and leave me alone.

I used to ask Nan questions about the spirits she openly talked to when going about her daily routine in the pub. I would ask, "Who are you chattering to now?"

"Just an old man called Sid, he was one of my regulars. A good fellow with a real sense of humour. He was tall with a large build and too talkative at times. I had to tell him to bugger off as he would get in my way."

Then we would laugh and I'd say, "You're a funny Nanny." I did not see Sid but I could smell him because he smoked Woodbines that were very strong. Nan said he chain smoked. So there was the smell of the Woodbines together with a musty smell when he was around.

Sid had died of a heart attack, dropped dead in the local cobbler's shop (shoe repairs). He lived alone so I think that he visited Nan for company. He went to the pub every day to find that certain company he enjoyed and knew he would find there, and so this continued after his death.

There was another regular person that went to the pub who had been widowed in the Second World War. A lady called Mrs Patricia Brown; she had had a double-barrelled surname, but after her husband had died she decided to drop the first part of it. She would come for a social drink on Friday and Saturday evenings and sit in the snug bar with her friend, another lady, the two of them drinking port and lemon together.

A quietly spoken lady, Nan said, "too good for the likes of this pub", a little posh. But they did like one another. After she died of pneumonia at the age of forty-two, customers said they could smell her perfume every now and then when you walked into the snug bar: Lily of the Valley. A couple of months before Patricia died she gave my Nan a piece of jewellery. It was an unusual brooch of a spider. I don't know the actual metal but it looked pewter, the body was a topaz stone. It looked old and really good, but I'm afraid I could never wear it, and so it's gone to a favourite niece of my Mum's in Canada. You have to be a certain kind of person to pin a large spider on your clothes; I always felt it was getting ready to jump. In other words, it gave me the creeps.

Little Georgie continued to visit the pub upstairs. I have already mentioned before the shock at having seen him in Nan's bedroom. Nan had said he was a dear boy with a sweet soul, and I shouldn't worry or be afraid of him. And I believed her. I never saw him again, but I could hear him giggle now and then.

And, of course, there was Nan's headless soldier in the cellar. When they were doing the Roman dig the pub's cellar wall was found to be connected to an adjoining wall which is said to be a soldiers' barracks. Nan spoke to the headless soldier for years, and she spoke about him to her customers, and yet she was so surprised that these men were unwilling to help her in the cellar.

As I mentioned before I did see entities in that pub. If I stood outside by the cellar door the air would be visible, as if the temperature had dropped below freezing. I would only go in there if someone else was with me. I have always enjoyed snooping around, but I could not find the courage this time to go in on my own. Once, when I was about six, an unearthly noise came out from beneath the cellar doors, and I made off like a rocket. Even to this day, I always jump out of my skin if I turn around and my husband or other family members are standing there. I always accuse them of doing it on purpose. I say to my husband, "Why do you have to sneak up on me like that?" He roars with laughter, "It's you! I called out your name!"

It's strange I never hear him or others in the family. Now if it's a spirit around me, I know instantly.

When I was about nine years old I was sitting on my own in the small sitting room; I was engrossed in reading a book, The Little Prince. I had received the book for prize giving day, and I felt very pleased with it. As a teacher had put me forward and chose it with me in mind, it had made me feel important. The sitting room was a few feet away from the cellar door, from the top level of the bar, down a flight of stairs. Then instinct made me look up and what I saw was something wide, I can only describe it as a floating grey coat with brass buttons, and then it disappeared. It had been diagonal and there was a musty smell that was left behind in the air for a few seconds, I never saw anything within the coat or around it.

Years later when they discovered the Roman

Painted House, my Nan Staveley said that they had found a headless body but I haven't been able to confirm that. I went along to speak with a few people on the site of the Roman Painted House and ask if they knew but they didn't. If anybody knows for sure I would love to know.

I can only say about the things that I have seen and experienced.

CHAPTER 5

The New Inn pub: inside but far away

The fog was clearing, and I could see again the cobbled stones beneath my feet. As I stumbled and swayed slightly, my mind was telling me that my right foot hit the small curb that went up onto the pavement. Regaining my composure I walked forward a few paces looking through the etched glass windows and reaching out to clasp hold of the handle at the front door of the pub. I had the sensation that I was pushing softly on the doors and they opened and I entered the pub. To my immediate right was the saloon bar with the walnut panelled walls and the swing door. A small room separated it from the public bar. The dividing walls and doors were only six feet in height, not reaching to the ceiling. There stood a small upright piano with a round wooden seat stool; its faded colours were of old burgundy and brown. There was also a small round oak table with cigarette stains on the rim edge and two matching little wooden chairs. Against the wall, beneath the window, was a lightweight pew for two. In fact, it had been quite a cosy snug room. Now there were long cobwebs and thick dust everywhere. The walls were an off cream colour due to all the smoking that had stained the previously white paint. Why was it so dusty and dirty? It was not like my Nan Staveley to let things slip like this, not to do her cleaning. It had been her mission in life to make everything look spotless and tidy. I walked on forward through the bar and the door opposite on the far left was closed. As I approached and then stood before it, the door opened towards me into the room. And so I carried on past, placing my foot onto the first step of the staircase that led up into the private sleeping quarters of the family. There was an eerie whistling noise only the wind can make that seemed to enclose me. I soon became aware that this was not a normal visit. I kept on climbing the stairs, looking ahead of me trying to see if I could see or hear anyone. Why was I feeling so very cold and alone? I had arrived at the top of the stairs.

"Jeanette," somebody was calling my name, "Jeanette, Jeanette," it continued in a soft voice. I wasn't able to reply.

'Where is my Mum and the rest of the family, where are they?' I wondered. I thought that I could smell lavender coming in small whiffs. I sensed my own fear but I kept on walking forward. I went into the first bedroom in which I normally slept with my parents, turning and coming on out again after seeing nothing: no furniture, nothing at all. The wooden floorboards were creaking but I continued, passing and peering into what was my Grandparents' room, and again nothing at all was in there.

I turned around and went to climb the stairs that led up to the two attic bedrooms. My whole body shook and my eyes were beginning to feel as though they were going to pop out of my head. Talking to myself and repeating the words, "Please no, don't make me go up there," but still I kept on walking and walked past the first open door and then on to the second bedroom and peered in. To my great surprise, there wasn't a monster inside. In fact, there were three small children staring at me with frightened looks on their faces. It felt freezing cold, looking at them I could see the air from their breath floating in front of their faces along with mine.

"Jeanette, Jeanette, you have to help us. Please come and find us."

I woke up with a start and thank goodness, I had been dreaming. But it all had seemed to be so real, that feeling of really being awake. I then become aware of just how cold I was, pulling the covers tightly up around me and sliding down further in the bed. The feelings of real fear I had, faded; we were going to Dover the coming weekend and I did not feel nervous but just a slight confusion about it all.

How very strange that all those years that I had stayed at the pub I had thought that there was something really bad in that room. There had been, only in a different way from I imagined.

Looking back now obviously they were premonitions, but why could I not have seen them coming in the years ahead and been able to do something about it? Of course, I was too young, being only about ten, to explain and who would have listened anyway?

All that I saw was dear little faces, but no names, no other information. I wasn't to know what that had all meant at the time but looking back realised the real truth and consequences of the Evil that was to come. God help us all.

These children would go missing and be murdered in the future. The faces of the three children would be known to the general public for the horrendous crimes of which they were the victims.

One little girl who went missing and was then found murdered had been taken from a funfair. The young boy who wore glasses has never been found. The other little girl was on her paper round. Again she was never found, only her bike had been left in a country lane.

One of these children I went to look for in June 2010, my darling daughter came with me. This will be related further on in my book.

My husband asked me a good question that you may be wondering too.

"Why would these children show themselves in that pub, when there wasn't any connection for them?"

My answer is ME, not the pub. I was the connection.

My psychic path has been to help children. Years later, in 2003, I started working for a group called Find Me. It began by looking for missing and murdered children, and then progressed to including adults.

CHAPTER 6

Mothers and daughters: a very sensitive child

As a child I loved my dolls and soft toys. If I kissed one more than the others, I felt it my duty to kiss them all again. They all slept in my bed with me. My mother said that I was too sensitive and silly to be her daughter. She had a strong character and was too complex a person for most people to understand, including me. A domineering woman, if the colour was white she would say that it was black. To say that she was an embarrassment at times would be a mild statement. I believe the fact that she was born into a large family of five living daughters made life very difficult for her. Nan might have been alright with me, but she did cause many upsets amongst her daughters and especially with my Mum.

When my Nan Staveley became ill with pneumonia and had to go into hospital, I went along with my mum to see her. At that time I was about ten years old.

It was in the afternoon, the weather was dreadful and raining hard. We came by the train from Ashford and by the time we had walked from the train station to Dover's Buckland Hospital we were soaked through.

The ward looked dreary and not very friendly. I said, "Hello, are you all right, Nan?" Anyone could see that she looked uncomfortable, and I wondered why she was shifting around so much in her bed.

"It's all these other people. I don't like them being here."

Mum went off to fetch a nurse.

"Can you see them, Jeanette?" asked my poor old Nan Staveley.

"How many of them can you see around you?"

"Three," was her reply.

I could see only one. I described the lady I was seeing in spirit.

"Oh, that is your great grandmother Jessie, my Mother. I have not seen her since she died, she has never shown herself to me. Do you suppose she has come for me, am I going to die?"

"I don't think so, Nan, you are just a bit poorly, that's all," I tried to comfort her.

"What's the matter, Mrs Staveley?" the nurse was asking in a severe tone.

"Off her head," my Mum was saying in a loud voice. "And this one's not much better," pointing at me, "I'm going for a cigarette." So off she went to the visitors' room; people were able to smoke in hospitals back then. I could feel my face going bright red and Nan was looking very intensely at me. The nurse probably thought we had shifty expressions, which we probably did. Nan said to me, "What's wrong, love?"

It was obvious that I felt uncomfortable, and I gave a nervous giggle. The cause, of course, was my Mum starting her performing to an audience around us, telling complete strangers certain personal things about us.

Before we left I whispered to Nan, "Am I really mad?"

With a certain expression on her face, "No, your Mother is."

That was the first time I saw Jessie in spirit, now when she comes, I just feel her. The sensation of heat goes right through me. I had two pictures of her in a frame on the wall in England, and I looked at her every day. Now they are packed in one of our boxes with other photos. Jessie was a sweet lady, and ended up dying in the New Inn pub. Mind you, Jessie never got on with her daughter, my Nan Rose, and this pattern continued with Rose and her daughter Coral and then Mum with me. But I can say in all honesty that I broke the mould with my lovely daughter, Lara. There is a God.........

There was another dependant for my Nan to take care of. It was Grandad Tom's mother, Agnes Rose, who was not as lucky as Jessie. She was born in Dover, lived there and expected to die there. Sadly, Nan Staveley was too weak at the time to continue looking out for her. She had her hands full with a heavy daily routine with the running of the pub.

Agnes Rose Staveley lived on the opposite side of the road in the Alms Houses, just up from the pub on York Street. When I first met her as a toddler, she frightened me so. This was probably because I had not seen such an old person before, and she was so very old and much wrinkled. Poor Agnes Rose ended up at a geriatric hospital near Ashford. It used to be the old Workhouse, and to think this brave old lady had been a nurse in the Crimean war. She received a medal for dedication and services to this country, and then went on to work as the Head Nurse for the Flour Mill in Riverside, Dover in Kent.

My Auntie Pam said that my Mum pinned Great Nan's medal onto her nightdress, so that the nurses would show her more respect. I was too young to visit her, but Mum did go twice a week. Part of her journey was on her bike and the rest by bus. It shows real dedication on her part, as it was a long way out of Ashford to travel.

I cannot say that I've seen my Mum cry that often in my life, and the first time was when Agnes Rose died. I don't think she ever forgave her own mother for putting her in the hospital. As for the precious medal, although it had been given to my Mum from Agnes Rose, it ended up with a family cousin in Canada and then somehow got to my Auntie Peggy who had it in her possession for years. When she died, it was returned to my mother for the last few years of her life. When my Mum died, I hoped to receive it, especially as I was a trained nurse, but we found out that she had given it away to strangers despite it having the surname Staveley on it: spitefulness on her part not to have offered it to me or to her only brother. I have to say that like a good many families, ours are not very compatible with each other. I do believe that Nan Staveley had a lot to do with this, passing on comments from one family member to another, which is such a shame.

One of the other times that I saw her cry was when my lovely stepfather, John, died. We hadn't seen them for eight years. Mum had stopped speaking to us over a silly incident in 1985. We had all gone to Germany: Mum and John in their car and Bob, me, Luke and Lara in ours. John made a mistake when driving; unfortunately the Police saw and followed us to our Motel. At the Motel Mum and John rushed inside quickly and because both cars were white the Police thought it was Bob who was the guilty party! Fortunately, they received a call and decided to let us go. Mum and John both refused to admit it was them that the Police were after and this caused an upset amongst us. So, when we returned to England Mum would not talk with us for eight years!

I discovered John was dying when I was visiting my Nan Staveley in Dover and she told me that John had a brain tumour. Apparently he had begged my Mum to contact me, as he wanted to see me, but she wouldn't. He was in the Hospice at Canterbury, Kent. When I arrived at the Hospice the staff said they did not know I existed, which was most distressing. They only had John's stepson, Edward my brother, on the list of family. When I went in to see him he broke down and cried and cried. He told me that he had missed me and wanted to see me so much. I hugged him and cried. I still feel such sadness that I cannot bear to talk about it. As I was driving away, Tina Turner was singing *Simply the Best* on the car radio, I've thought about him every time I've heard that song since then.

He died the next day. I was with him and Mum when he died early in the morning and was able to help Mum. I took her back home to Dover and wanted to stay with her, but she refused. Possibly she needed to cry alone as she couldn't accept he had gone. Poor Mum.

CHAPTER 7

Family and friends: my teenage years

As I grew up and understood a little more about the voices and the visions life took on a different meaning. It wasn't always a better one, just a bit strange.

My Mum had her own demons to contend with, so we never had any meaningful conversations, right up to her death. It was my Mum's way to give me a doll to keep me amused rather than give me her time. To be fair to her, around that period she had been working hard seasonally picking hops, strawberries and potatoes. She started hop picking with my Dad's Mum Nan Wilder in all the hop gardens around Kent with other locals and those from London. We were taken with her and Nan before we were old enough for school. One year she decided no more field work and took on a cleaning job until later on she started work at the local Rimmel's factory on the conveyor belt packing the make-up products. She would bring home seconds: make-up that wasn't good enough to be sold. Then she'd invite the neighbours' girls round and let them have their pick and I had what was left. Another example of her showing off to outsiders and a bit meanly giving me the scraps.

Like a lot of women she didn't have much time left over at the end of a working day. And so I would go and look for my little Nan Wilder to talk with. Also Nan Staveley when we visited my Grandparents at Dover, not that I understood much of what she talked about.

When Mum was older she learnt a new skill and became a welder in a factory teaching men. Looking back, that was quite something in those days.

One funny memory of Mum that I have was going into the town after her work was finished and going to a cafe/restaurant called Gizzi's, run by an Italian family. We used to have a cup of tea and a crusty white buttered roll with a bag of plain crisps. It made me feel happy. I especially recall the day Mum told me off for talking whilst eating and then did exactly what I did and choked on her roll, coughing loudly and going red in the face. I could not help her for laughing, thinking that could have been me. Her embarrassment was such we never went back for a month. Unfortunately, the first words on our return were, "How are you today, Mrs Wilder, feeling better?" Naturally, Mum had thought they wouldn't remember the incident. I giggled and walked off to find us a table.

I think I secretly enjoyed her being uncomfortable rather then it being me for a change. Haaaah!

The saying....... God works in mysterious ways.........

Three days after my fifteenth birthday started out being no different to any other day. It was to be a quite devastating day for our family, especially for me.

I heard Mum speaking to my Dad in the sitting room and so I walked in to see them both. Mum stood there with her coat on and a packed suitcase beside her on the floor. I will always remember her saying, "Ron, I won't go if you don't want me to." My Dad did not say a word, just stared straight ahead. "Mum, what are you saying?" I said. All she said was, "I am leaving you all," and with that she walked out the door. Outside was a parked car with a dark haired man sitting inside. Mum walked past Ed and got into the car and they drove off. Ed and I went back inside the house and stood in front of Dad, who said just, "Your mother's gone, go to your rooms." It was such a shock, who on earth was that man and why didn't Dad try and reason with her? I sobbed for hours; I don't know about Ed as he would not let me in his bedroom or speak to me.

The next day we all went to see Nan and Grandad Wilder. Dad went in the garden to talk with Grandad and then Ed followed them out. I stayed with my Nan. Apparently, Mum had already spoken to Nan about leaving us and it came as no surprise to my Grandparents. "Don't worry Jeanie, it will be alright," she tried to comfort me. It wasn't, though. Those following months were very sad for me as I lost all confidence in myself.

In those days it was a bit of a scandal when one of a couple left their family, and I felt this awful shame of it. It turned out that she had told everyone, the neighbours and the women she worked with, that as soon as I was fifteen and left school she would be off. So everyone knew what she was going to do but us. My Mum always had an evil streak in her and must have thought it was funny.

Before she left, Mum had seen an advert in the paper for a live-in mother's help and rang the lady up. She then told me, and arranged with Mrs Dow to meet at the Market Inn in Lower Bank Street in Ashford. Mrs Dow seemed a nice middle class lady who wanted someone to help with her three children and do chores about the home. So it was agreed that I should start working for her in six months time when I became fifteen and a half. Until then her mother was helping her with the children. Having done this, my Mum clearly felt free to leave.

After my Mum left, my Dad withdrew from us and was drinking more. He did not take charge of the home at all. Ed and I weren't given any direction in what to do. The house became a mess. There was hardly any food in, and I don't remember Dad cooking anything for us. Ed was working and going to Nan's for his lunch. I tried cleaning the house but got a nasty response from Ed, who made it clear he did not want me around. It had turned cold being autumn time, and I would dress myself up in the coat that she had left behind. It was in light felt wool, three quarter length and what is called a dog tooth check in a pale green and cream. It was a bit too old in style and too big in size for me really, but that did not bother me as I hadn't got a coat at that time that fitted me.

I had started going more and more to my friends, and it was their Mums who fed me. I would go to my

Nan's just for a short visit as Grandad was put out by the attention that Nan was giving me. So up until his death I spent more and more time with my friend Glynis. She was having quite a hard time of it with her Mum too, but we had become good friends at the secondary school, being in the same class. Glynis had wanted to be a dancer but her mother had said no.

Glynis showed me how to do tight curls on the top of the head, using one forefinger on both hands to curl the hair around the fingers and pull them out without losing the curl and put a hair clip in to secure the hair. She did mine and then I would do hers for her. My hair was very dark brown and hers was a light mousey brown. The boys told us we were both very pretty girls, which was flattering for us both. We bought black cotton and chiffon material and her Mum made us identical dresses to wear to the country village hall dances. I stayed overnight quite often with her until she got a job up in London. Previously, when we first left school, we went along to sit for the same job as a clerk in a small office called Hedley's, which was a printing firm for books. I had been hoping to do this work rather than being a mother's help. The shop was in the high street of the town. Neither of us got the job: we were copying each other's work and giggling. Afterwards, we went to a shop called Dolce which was a small shoe shop. For a few weeks we had been begging our Dads to buy us a pair of gaiters to go over our black shoes and now they were ours. I think my Dad agreed because of guilt for not looking after me; they were one of only two presents that he ever bought me. Still, these were fabulous: black leather with a black fluffy trim around the top that came just below the knees and a black strap that went under the sole and slipped over a button on the edge of the side of the black shoe. We felt like the bee's knees.

Then Glynis got herself a job as a mother's help in London and wanted me to go up there with her. There was another family who lived close by and also needed someone. This was in the 60s. Dad refused to let me go.

Before my Mum left my Dad was an overprotective father who would tell boys to clear off from our garden gate when they were just being friendly and talking with me. On one occasion, I was at a music evening for young people in a small hall a couple of streets away, with my friend Greek Stella (she was called this because her Mum was Greek). Just after eight o'clock, my Dad turned up because I was ten minutes late and ordered me out of the hall. I had to sit on his push bike as he pushed me up the road. I felt silly and embarrassed as all my peers were outside watching all this. It was the last time I went. I was fourteen at the time. After Mum had gone it was as if I didn't exist, but he still made a point of putting his foot down saying I could not go to London.

By this time I had made up my mind to start searching for my Mum who had gone back to her home town, Dover. Not a word did we hear from her, until I found out she had contacted my brother Ed, but not me, and had invited him for Christmas. Nan gave me some money for the train fare, and after several weeks of searching and the upset of not knowing where she was I found her. Years later I did wonder if I should have left well alone and not have bothered, but still, she was my Mum. This day I caught the five o'clock train from Ashford to Dover Priory station. My Mum had worked as a barmaid before in Nan Staveley's pub and I don't know what made me try this time and not before but I walked into the Dover Priory pub just outside of the station and there she was.

Staring at me, she then said, "What are you doing here?"

I replied, "I thought that I would come and look for you."

She wasn't too happy seeing me. "Go on up to Nan's and see if she will put you up for the night."

"How about later Mum, when you have finished work?"

"No, John and I are going out." (John ended up being our stepfather) "We go to parties on a Saturday night, so off you go now, you are not old enough to come into a pub on your own. Here's some money. Get a taxi there, and go back to Ashford tomorrow."

So I left the pub and walked towards the town. I could hear some noise and loud music coming from Pencestor Park, which is in the centre of the town: a fair had come to town, with lots of rides and plenty of excited young people there. I walked in through the park and over towards the Big Wheel and stood by the railings. There were a few girls around my age group standing and chatting. One of the girls was a ginger haired girl who introduced herself to me as Judy Abbott. I called myself Janie, I can't think why except I felt like pretending to be someone else. She asked if I would like to go on the Big Wheel with her as the others didn't want to. I agreed, and this was a start of a new friendship which lasted until I became seventeen and stopped going down to Dover. She turned out to be a lovely person and a good friend with a kind family who just invited me into their home without knowing what sort of person I was or anything about me.

That night I ended up at my Grandparents after dark, knocking on the prefab door, "Hello, can I come in?" Nan put me to bed and I could hear Grandad moaning about it in the next bedroom. I had walked for half an hour through the dark streets which took me out a long way from the centre of the town and up the hilly climb into the Buckland estate. On the way a man came out from a pub and was walking alongside me for a while before turning down another road. He spoke to me, "What are you doing so young walking the streets this late at night?" He was right, as nobody would have known where I was to look for me if I had gone missing. Looking back, I put myself in many dangerous situations by quite often doing this sort of thing without thinking things through. I had spent the money for the taxi on the fair ride and a bag of chips with Judy.

I didn't give up trying to see my Mum. One Saturday evening Judy's Dad gave me a lift in his car to Mum's flat: she had recently moved to the Buckland estate just two streets up above where my Grandparents lived. He waited with Judy whilst I knocked on the front door. Mum answered and said that they were going to a cocktail party and that I could not come in or stay with them for the night. I must have looked distressed because Mr Abbott got out of the car, took my arm and said, "Right, you are coming back with us, get in the car." He never spoke a word to my Mum. Again, strangers took care of me. I have been so fortunate that kind people helped me through such difficult periods in my life.

In the New Year, when I started working for the Dow family, my Mum and John came up from Dover in his car to take me out to Woodchurch, where the family lived. After the introductions, they stayed for about twenty minutes then they left me with strangers and went off.

That night I cried myself to sleep. That experience of abandonment, of rejection, stays with a person for most of their lives. In the two and a half years that I lived with the Dow family my Mum rang twice, and my previously overprotective Father never once came out to see where I was. More importantly, he never met any of the family I worked and lived with.

I was fifteen and a half when I went to live and work in the country just outside a village called Woodchurch, a few miles from the town of Ashford. I moved in with a good family as a live-in mother's help, looking after three children and taking care of the cleaning of their home. Except for a remark from the precocious six year old, I felt comfortable living there. "You have got to do this, you are our servant," said Ann, which silenced and shocked me, especially coming from a small child.

The lady of the house was the daughter of long-standing wealthy farmers who farmed nearby. Her husband worked for the Ashford Courts. They were a middle class family and mine came from working class. Their bungalow was also a small farm holding, with eggs and chickens to sell and the growing of vegetable produce and plants.

I was asked if I could cook. I replied, with honesty, "No, not really." I did try. I made some really horrible lumpy custard and so they never asked me again. Mary continued cooking the meals along with a very heavy workload throughout her day. She really was a nice person, but firm.

One day, quite out of the blue, they asked if I could spend some time outside helping them get the chickens ready for a customer, as they were behind with the order. They were surprised that I refused the job of breaking the chicken's necks!

I declined but with a rather high pitched voice, "I think not," squalling at the top of my voice, "How dare you expect me to commit murder!"

Looking shame faced they crept out of the bungalow rather sheepishly. They returned a few hours later with big smiles saying, "How are we feeling now?" obviously hoping for the sweet-natured girl that I usually was. There I was, still with the look of thunder on my face! I heard Roy saying "Oh bugger!"

Years later they said that I had prepared them for the dreaded teenage stage of their three children! Still, they also said that I had been the nicest girl, - sensible, trustworthy and clean (with the emphasis on CLEAN) - that had lived with them.

I used to say to Dad and Nan, "I keep finding money in very obscure places - under mats and beds, all so odd!"

Dad asked me, "What did you do with it?"

"Oh, I told them that I had found it and put it on the kitchen window sill."

"Good girl, they are only testing you, to see if you are an honest person to have living in their home."

When I had some free time after the housework was finished for the day, I did help them out planting seedlings, which I enjoyed doing. Being able to run your fingers through the earth is so wonderful. I would creep out to the greenhouses, especially when the baby was fast asleep outside in his pram and in the sunshine. I helped them with the selling of their fresh eggs, vegetables and plants when passing trade knocked at the door. People would say, "Are you Sandie Shaw's sister? You look just like her!" which rather pleased me. Many girls had a similar look, but it was still nice to hear it.

The highlight of my life then was once a week when a Mr Wilson from the town of Tenterden would arrive in his grey van. He had a large frame but was of medium height. Mr Wilson was a likeable, extremely talkative character, who was expected to pass on any information he had gleaned on his route. He had tinned foods, biscuits, cakes, newspapers, magazines and sweets. Once a month I would receive my Rave magazine, which had all the latest pictures of pop stars. The Rolling Stones were my favourite group, but George Harrison was the one I loved. I had his photo in a picture frame which went everywhere with me. I got asked if he was my boyfriend by little Ann. Smiling, I would make a funny noise, "mm, mm," thinking 'I wish!'

There was lots of interest in the fresh-faced models like Jean Shrimpton and Twiggy. The clothes were great as there were only a few of each design. Yes, everyone had the fashion look, but you could find things that were so different in small boutiques. All of this was so new then, and it was great trying to get a certain look but also be unique. I was so proud of being able to save money and clothe myself at fifteen and a half.

Each week I spent a lot of my money on sweets. Mr Wilson would remark. "How come you're so skinny after eating so much?" I felt smug. I don't feel so smug now!

When I told the Dow family that I was leaving to start nursing they were relieved, as they had been wondering how to say to me they were letting me go. This was because they would have to start to pay me more money when I was eighteen. I left at eighteen to go and work at the hospital, but left with a new Nurse's watch they bought me as a parting gift. They were such a lovely family and taught me so much about having aspirations in life.

Again neither parent checked out the hospital or Nurses' Home. The only time Dad visited me was one evening with Uncle Erne in his car. They had both been drinking. They went to the pub at the top of the lane which was the local pub which the nurses and doctors would go to. Dad came staggering down to the Nurses' Home, which was called Pine Trees, to be met by a Miss Taylor who proceeded to tell him off. We all had our exams in the morning, so she wasn't going to let him see me but relented after speaking with me, "An hour only, Miss Wilder!"

I am leaving out so many things as it is all too

much. The big thing that stands out in my mind was when I became ill at work, and they said I should go home for a week. They did not know about my situation back there, but I did go home. I arrived back at Cryol Road and went to my bedroom to discover my brother Ed had taken it over. My bed was still there, now Ed's, but all my personal things were gone. My Dad had given my big dolls to a family; I never knew who had them. My clothes, books, anything personal had gone, put out for the dustman. My cuddly toys, including my favourite two monkeys, my two pretty bridesmaid dresses - a lovely mauve and a pale blue with a netted overlay - were gone. How I had loved those dresses! Even my beloved bike that I spent hours of solitary time on had gone from the shed. So my brother had my room, my bed and my Mum had come when nobody was there and taken my dressing table and the glass table set that she had previously given to me.

My brother's bed had been thrown out and there was only one piece of furniture that was left in my brother's room, a small child's writing desk that had been Ed's. In fact, it is still in the family today as my Grandchildren own it. So, there I was in a small box bedroom and no bed. I found some old bedding and made a bed on the floor. I left a note downstairs to say that I was upstairs. I felt very poorly with the virus and slept quite a lot over a few days. I would get up and make the odd cup of tea and a sandwich of bread and butter to eat. Not what my supervisors had in mind when they sent me home to be cared for!

Funny recalling these things, as I had never felt any bitterness towards my Dad, maybe a little bit cross, but really just so sad. I expect when he looked back over his life he must have realised what he failed to do for us all. But I loved him dearly.

My Dad never did buy me another bed to sleep on or help me paint or wallpaper the room. I had hoped that I could move back when I had time off from my training over the next couple of years and needed a break from the Nurses' Home. I remember a few months later buying some white paint and some large checked orange material for curtains. Disaster struck as I had bought the wrong type of paint for walls, and the curtains only just reached across the opening but the light still shone through it. Nan Wilder had lent me the money to buy a divan single bed. Bless her heart, as she had little money herself. I started now and again staying there but gave up in the end. My poor room stayed the same until in the eighties when my husband and I moved Dad into a flat. I gave the divan bed to Nan to have in her small lounge in the bungalow, where she eventually ended up sleeping.

Looking back my Dad really did nothing for me, but then he didn't do much for poor little Nan before and especially after Grandad died. He should have mowed her lawns, cleaned her windows and spoilt her now and then. But he didn't. I did it for years even after I married. Then a few years later, she got a nice old man called Mr Gray to do odd jobs and the gardening. Dad never liked him, probably due to a mixture of jealousy and guilt since he knew that he could have done all these jobs for his mother.

Working for the Dow family between these years, I met Margaret when I was seventeen. She was a pretty girl with long blond hair and was several years older than myself. We started going out at weekends when I had finished working at Saturday lunch time. We caught a bus to Ashford and sometimes a train to different places like Folkestone and Maidstone. We met many young lads; everything was so innocent in those days! We spent our time walking around the harbour and strolling on the beach, buying whelks and cockles from the many stalls.

Occasionally we went to the coffee shop for our frothy coffee and listened to the music on the jukebox. There was a permanent fair on the seafront with many rides and an arcade which had games with money slot machines. It was all so lively with families on holiday from around the country. With Margaret I started going to see bands in Kent. She became friends with Richard who was in a famous group The Fortunes; Richard had come from Ashford. After that we started to go to the different venues where they played. I was earning my own money then and was able to pay my way and buy my own clothes. Today my wage would be two pounds and fifty pence as a live-in Mother's help! I felt quite grown up at seventeen.

Out of my two Grandads, Grandad Staveley died first and I was told over the phone, but I was not invited to the funeral. That was when I was sixteen. It was a great upset to me as Grandad and I had built a good relationship between us. On a Saturday evening Nan and he used to go on the bus to an old pub called The Mogul in Dover, and if I arrived he would always say, with mock reluctance, "Oh well, we're stuck with you now, be quick and put your coat on again or we'll miss the bus." He would treat me to a glass of bitter lemon and a packet of plain crisps that had a small dark blue packet containing salt, allowing you to put as much or little as you wanted on the crisps then shake them to mix the salt. I loved being with them. I would just watch and listen to their conversations and old Grandad swearing, waving his hands in the air and laughing. Then after a couple of hours we walked to the bus station and caught the last bus back up to the Buckland estate. He said that he dreaded a Sunday, with Nan's terrible attempts at cooking a roast dinner and me demanding to watch Ready Steady Go. The programme was directed at young people, with dancing and all the famous groups, and was very loud. All he wanted to do on a Sunday was watch cricket on the television and take a nap, poor Grandad. Unfortunately, what I ended up inheriting from him was his illness of bronchial asthma when I was twenty-two years old which changed my life forever.

Then shortly afterwards, my American Grandad, Bud Wilder, his full title was Franklyn Sterrett Wilder, died. It was all so awful: my Dad rang me at the family of Mr and Mrs Dow and said that he had passed away, after a massive heart attack which had been two days earlier. My poor little Nan. After the phone call I walked all the way back to Ashford to be with her, which took me over two hours. After his funeral I tried to spend as much time as possible with her at weekends.

From the age of fifteen until I married at twenty there had been a wonderful group of people around me. I never saw Judy and her parents, or Glynis ever again. I never returned to visit the Dow family either although I had been so close to their baby, Mark; I did see Mary and Roy separately on rare occasions in the town. When the door closed, I never went back. But wasn't I such a lucky girl? I had a positive happy disposition and I was fit and healthy then. More than anything in the world I had my darling little Nan. I thought that I had taken it all in my stride and never realised some of my misfortunes. What more could I have asked for? Absolutely nothing.

But my husband says that I had sadness in my eyes and he doesn't like to look at my earlier photos as it makes him feel upset for me. He knows me better than anyone.

Others can see things that we are not always aware of ourselves.

CHAPTER 8

My dear little Nan: Gertrude Ann Wilder

Little Nan was my Dad's mother. She was a good friend and mentor, like a true mum to me. I really loved her and the feeling was mutual. I have to be honest and say she wasn't always nice to my own Mum and Auntie, but that was between them. In her eyes they just did not live up to what she wanted for her sons.

When I was a young child she and Grandad would come for Christmas at our house. Watching the television, Nan was always talking to me and holding my hand. The others in the room would get irritated by this and kept saying, "Be quiet!" as if we were in the pictures or the library, and I would giggle and say, "You like nattering don't you Nan?" Then we would both be told off.

Nan was with me with all the traumas that happened to me and I with her. She helped me when I was ten years old and I had had a terrible accident at school. I had climbed over the stone wall at school to get a girl's ball back. Another girl had thrown it over by mistake and they were arguing about who should get it. It was typical of me that I said, "I'll get it!"

I climbed over onto the waste land and then I stood on a rusty iron pram handle and it sprang up and slit my left leg right across above the knee. It was so deep you could see the inner layer of the dermis that was orange and just pinpricks of blood were coming through. Everyone went quiet and stared at me, but I managed to get myself back over and hobbled into the head mistress's office. The poor teacher who was in the office with Miss Scott at the time nearly fainted when she saw it. They called for a taxi and this teacher came to Accident and Emergency with me. It is as clear today as it was all those years ago how frightened I was and how much it hurt having those stitches put in.

That evening Mum said, "Well I can't do anything now as I am off to Dover to see my parents," with which she swanned off in her best clothes for the weekend without a thought of how I would be. I slept in with my Dad that night and the next day I was poorly and went to see my Nan for some comfort. By the end of the day I was covered in a bright red rash which was itchy and sore. Nan paid for a taxi which took my Dad and me up to Ashford Hospital where they diagnosed that I was allergic to penicillin. They gave me antihistamine tablets for the itching and put calamine lotion all over me and sent me home. I stayed with Nan and Grandad that night, and she made me a bed on the settee and a cup of sweet tea with a couple of pieces of toast. The next day I went back with my Dad to our home at Cryol road. Mum returned home on the Sunday evening and I don't recall anything nice to say.

Off to Nan's for the weekends was something that I always was grateful for: love, peace and fun. When I had finished at the Dows' at midday on a Saturday I would walk up the lane to the main road to catch the bus that would take me on my journey back to Ashford. The bus only came twice a day so if I missed it then it was a long walk home, about twelve miles in all. Quite often I would hitch-hike home, I never told Nan or my Dad!

My suitcase in one hand and a lettuce in the other, I would arrive at my Nan's front door. "Hello Nan, it's me." She would always say, "Who is me?"

Nan's home was my home but only after my grandfather had died. He loved me but was a little jealous of my special relationship with Nan; he was a bit possessive of Nan. I did not mind because they adored one another.

Nan was a character, a typical looking Nan with a short straight haircut with a section of the hair at the front twisted into a curl, secured with a clip of some description in the day. At night she would put a metal clip into this section of hair at the front to put a wave into it. The clip was big and nasty looking. She could not lie on her side in bed as it would stick into her forehead but it was a sacrifice she made for the curl. Something which used to make me laugh was that if there was thunder and lightning she would carry on nattering until I took it out.

"Quick take the thing out, there's a good girl. I will

be struck by lightning and die."

"What in bed, Nan?"

Sometimes my feet would touch hers and quite often she would shout at me about how cold my feet were.

"They are like blocks of ice, take them off me!"

Poor old Nan had me in fits of laughter. "It's not funny Jeanie," she would say as she was trying not to laugh.

The six corks tied together on some wool were the best of all, what a mystery that was! She kept them by her feet in the bottom of the bed and more often than not I would get my feet entangled in them.

Then she would mutter "Be careful, I need them."

"Why are they in bed with us Nan?"

"They are supposed to help with the bunions on my feet."

"Oh that's a good one." They never did improve her feet.

The very best of all was her rubber truncheon she kept by her bed, placed on the top of her commode.

"It's just in case we get an intruder so we can defend ourselves."

"What would you do first, Nan?" trying to sound serious.

"Would you say 'Hang on a minute please whilst I take out my clip so I look respectable', or 'I need some help to get to my feet and get untangled from the wool and corks', then ask them to hand you the truncheon? Then just mention 'Bend down as I wish to hit you over the head with it.' "

"Oh you," she would giggle.

I called her little Nan as she was only five feet one

inch tall and I am five feet six, but you didn't want to get on the wrong side of her. The look that she would give if you did anything wrong was enough to make you curl up and want to die.

She was as bright as a button and loving with a good sense of humour but also very naughty. She would share her last piece of bread and butter with me, and a quarter of a pound of mince would spread between four adults.

One particular day she had made a cottage pie for my Dad, brother and the two of us. Well, what a calamity it was, it slipped from my hands as I took it out of the oven!

"Quick, scoop it up before they get back from the pub. They won't know the difference," said Nan.

They did enjoy it. "Are you two not hungry then?" as they both looked inquiringly at us, knowing that we both loved our food.

"No," we said, "We had a bun with a cup of tea earlier and it must have taken the edge off our appetite".

A twinkle in her eye, she whispered to me, "When they have gone we will have a boiled egg and soldiers."

I laughed out loud.

My brother Ed said, "What's the matter with her?"

We never did tell them.

Trudy was her name, and she was a real darling to me. Without her I would not have survived as well as I had in my early years. The rejected feelings that I had from my Mum went away when I was with her.

So it was a natural thing to do, inviting my boyfriends to her house. Some of them were quite strange.

One of my strange boyfriends was a hard man, a fighter, not my type at all but I could not say no when he asked me out on a date. He turned up in a pinstriped suit. Dad answered the door and let him in to the sitting room. Dad was looking very displeased and hovered over him. He was my height, not very tall for a man.

Dad later said, "I thought that I was letting the Mafia boss of Ashford take my little girl out on a date."

Nan, as usual, was scrutinising him and out popped the question, "Haven't you got beautiful teeth?"

My thoughts: 'Oh my, here we go, Nan and her questions.'

"Nan, don't ask or say personal things."

"Why? she said.

"They are false," he responded, "My own, they were knocked out in a fight."

I thought Nan was going to pass out. Sitting back down and saying, "Oh, goodness me, fancy that!" Looking at her son, "Ron, what do you think of that?"

Dad said nothing but was looking angry.

I said in a rush, "Shall we go then?"

My Dad said, "Make sure you are home by 10pm."

My date looked down at my legs: I was wearing long white socks as they were fashionable then. He looked quite baffled, and he refused to walk alongside of me because of the long white socks. I suppose it did not go with his image and so I walked behind him. After that evening, we decided we were not suited!

Then there was the unfortunate James. James, oh poor James, he did not know what he was letting himself in for, going out with me!

I met him one cold and frosty evening at the local espresso coffee bar, named Tiffany's. Yes, I know, but that is the true name, ask any of the veterans of the town from 1966. It was full of young people, and very smoky and loud. The noise came from excited chattering and the Rolling Stones and Beatles music blaring out from the jukebox that was just inside beside the front door.

This was the hip place to be, er, the only place at that time open in the evenings, other than the multitude of pubs in the small market town. What was so impressive about James was his scooter, which was parked outside. He owned the fastest amongst the group of young men. It was big, shiny and green. This gave him an edge, if only a small one.

He was nothing much to look at, but seemed pleasant and grateful to have a girlfriend. Three months in all was long enough on my part, although riding on the back of his scooter was good. Mostly because of all the attention it attracted; it made me feel so like a 60s pop singer - in my mind only, of course. We did not have to wear helmets as it wasn't the law at that time. I would pull on one of my fashionable hats or tie a chiffon scarf around my hair trying to imitate Audrey Hepburn. It was all such an exciting time for the young.

He wore cream Bri-Nylon shirts that showed off a very hairy chest beneath it. He obviously thought I should find this attractive. Unfortunately, it made me cringe.

He went off one week with his mate on a biking holiday to Wales. He rang me as soon as he returned, extremely excited; he had missed me very much and wanted to show me his holiday slides.

"OK, how about this Saturday at my Nan's bungalow?"

"Fine, that's a date."

Five o'clock in the evening on the dot, in he came with bundles of equipment. He set about putting it all up in the front room. Nan and I sat quiet and demure on the couch for a long time before Nan started fidgeting.

Whispering, "When is he going to get on with it?"

I shushed at her, "Be quiet, Nan, he'll hear you."

Another half hour passed and he was still twittering on.

Nan said, "I can't bear this Jean, it's getting me down."

It was one thing to ask my Nan to sit and listen, but to expect her not to want to talk was another thing. "My throat is dry and I need a cup of tea!" she declared. The next thing that happened was the turning point of my relationship with the poor James.

He was oblivious to Nan's moaning and my shushing as he was on a roll with a captive audience. Nan stood up and this almighty sound came from her bottom. I felt shocked and went bright red, and James stopped in his tracks. This little voice said, "Oh dear, was that me?" She snatched up her walking stick and I had never seen her move as fast as she did then. It was as if she was on wheels, but on every move escaped another fart. It wasn't heard of then, people were more graceful and you didn't even *speak* of bodily functions in nice company.

I felt so ashamed, I did not look or speak to James, I was dumbstruck. I rushed past him like a whirlwind, hurtling into the kitchen and slamming the door shut behind me. Trapped together, Nan said, "Do you think he would like a nice cup of tea?"

I was mortified. In a high pitched voice I said, "No, it isn't any good pretending to be genteel after that performance."

I was beside myself. I wasn't going out there for anybody. We both shared a nervous giggle, which had got us into lots of trouble before and this was no exception.

Ears pressed to the kitchen door we could hear him taking all the equipment down again, gathering it all together and quietly leaving the bungalow without a word, only the click of the door when it shut. By the time he closed the front door behind him, the height of giggling hysteria could be heard.

Afterwards Nan said, "I'm glad he's gone, he bored me to death. Let's have a cake and a slice of bread and butter with our tea." Obviously, the trauma had made her hungry.

"Don't bring him here again Jean; I could not face it."

Staring her straight in the eye, "*You* couldn't?!"

So that was that, poor James was history………..

But when my Nan first saw my husband as he walked up the path in his suit she said, "I like the look of him," and so his fate was sealed. Nan ended up loving him; she would say 'good old Bob'. The feeling was mutual.

I do mention this quite a bit throughout my story: like

my Nan, I had a nervous giggle. I must have inherited it from her. We were hopeless together in some situations, especially if it was a serious one. For example, Nan was invited to her grandniece's wedding at the main Catholic Church in Ashford. She asked me to go with her. My husband said that he would look after our baby son, Luke, so I could go. Nan wore a grey skirt with a white blouse, a pale pink cardigan with a pretty brooch. And a strange looking pink hat.

"Are you sure about that hat, Nan?" The net was a bit scrunched up at the front and it seemed out of shape. I started laughing.

"It's fine," she said, as she was getting fidgety waiting for the taxi to arrive.

"I'm glad it's on your head and not mine." We clashed in colours as I wore a red mini skirt with small white polka dot spots, and a cream cheesecloth blouse with unusual sleeves. My husband said that I looked pretty, laughing, "Shame about your Nan's hat." Off we went to the church, the odd couple. We entered the church late and, trying to be quiet, sat in the back row. The service had already started. Everybody looked round and stared as we shuffled in.

As anyone knows a Catholic service goes on and on, plus you end up getting a lecture from the Priest in how to behave. So in the end, the poor Catholic girls think that Christ is going to be sitting there on the bed watching you on your wedding night. This amused us and so we started to giggle and giggle, sliding lower and lower, trying to hide beneath the top of the pew. We got louder and louder, and the church went quiet as the bride and groom signed the register. I suggested maybe we should make a break for it as the giggles were getting uncontrollable and both of us were flushed in the face, "Let's get out of here Nan."

Thinking about it some more, I said, "Wait until the bride and groom leave."

"No, Jean, I've got to go now, with all that laughing I need the bathroom."

And so we did. With Nan with her walking stick it was not the kind of exit that we hoped for. Instead of a quick retreat, it became slow and painful. We had pre-booked the taxi for an hour to pick us up again from outside of the church and luckily it was waiting. We got in and I said to the taxi driver, "Put your foot down," and so we roared off, leaving the relatives looking bemused.

Looking back, we probably did behave quite badly. A week later her niece Olive, the bride's mum, visited Nan. She told us they heard the giggling and that she could see only my hand gripping the pew and that hat. "Why did you leave so soon?" she asked, "Oh, and by the way, I have a message from Father Woods. He wonders how long has it been since your last confessions?"

We both sighed and replied, "Oh dear."

When I was sixteen, my Nan gave me some money to go up to Ashford to buy a suitcase for her. It was lovely: white with a baby blue lining. The only trouble was I loved it, so it became mine. Nan only got to use it twice, when she left her bungalow to visit with her eldest son who lived in Berkshire. And so on these rare occasions she would ask if she could use her own suitcase. Very begrudgingly I parted with it. Nan gave up in the end and surrendered it to me, on the condition she could use it if she needed it. And so I happily agreed. It became a very special possession of mine.

I guess it made me feel important carrying it about, back and forth at weekends from my live-in job in the country. When I was seventeen, I saved to buy a grey cape that had a black trim and you had to put your arms through slits in the front. It looked smart and fashionable, but I felt frozen when the weather turned cold. Nan's words of wisdom were 'Always make sure you keep your shoes in good repair and polished.', 'Never go out in laddered stockings or tights.' and 'Look after your hair, it is your crowning glory.' I've never forgotten those words. I remember it as if it was yesterday.

I continued to use the case when I started nursing. I lived in several nurses' homes, five in all, until I finished my training. And when I got married it also went on honeymoon with us. Now it houses lots of our family photos. But I do know the real reason behind me wanting it so badly: it represented a blanket comforter. I knew my Nan loved me unconditionally, as I did her, and I felt that she was not far from me when I could see that lovely white suitcase.

Nan had guided me towards nursing, and was so pleased and proud that I became a Registered Nurse. She would always tell me, "You are a good, kind clever girl, my Jeanie, with such a gentle touch." Alas, once I nipped her finger when cutting her nails. She hooted at me, "That hurt!"

"Well, you should have kept still instead of waving your hands about," I cried. I only did it the once in twenty-five years but she would raise it every time! I would wash her hair and put grips to hold it and make a curl at the front, as she liked it. Then I'd wash her feet, cut the nails and massage her legs. She did enjoy that so much.

My darling Nan has been gone since 1988 but will always be with me. I miss her so. I had a party on the Saturday, and my oldest friend Julie was with me when I received a phone call that Nan was poorly and wanted me to visit her at the nursing home she had moved into, just ten minutes away. Leaving Julie to help my husband with the guests, I went to see Nan. I asked the staff to arrange for the doctor to see her and said I would be back in the morning. She died two days after my fortieth birthday.

My little Nan Wilder, we shared so many special times together. I always had my Nan in my life. I was the one with her when she died. Her two sons were told to go to the waiting room and stay there for further news, but I refused to go anywhere else. I knew she didn't have long to live, and so I clung on to her hand when they moved her upstairs from the Accident and Emergency department. I told the doctor not to stick needles in her; I wanted her to be able to pass over peacefully now that her time had come. She would not have come back as Nan anyway, with what had taken place within her brain. But they never relayed my wishes to the staff up on the ward. I was still holding Nan's hand when they pushed the trolley into the lift and managed to run over my foot. I went limping with her towards the ward where the Sister insisted I stood outside the ward of six beds. "Let us make her comfortable and then you can come in."

I had waited a few minutes when the alarm went and all was noise and confusion. It was one of the saddest moments in my life, and almost unbearable to watch. Even though I have been part of a resuscitation team myself, I was so angry when they got to her before me and bounced her twice before I managed to grab the Doctors' arms, shouting for them to stop. They had not received the information not to resuscitate. She was ninety-one and had had enough and wanted to be with her late husband, her son Frank who was killed in the Second World War and her sister Olive (Ollie).

I held her hands for an hour and in my head I was calling, 'Nanny, please my Nanny, please don't leave me.' But as I quietly wept I knew that she had to go. I was crying for my loss. The air went very cold then a nurse popped her head in through the curtains. "Are you alright my dear? Gosh, it feels really cold in here."

"I'm alright. I want to stay a while longer please."

My Dad and Uncle knew nothing of what went on, I had made all the decisions about Nan to the end. Afterwards I went home and climbed into my bed and my lovely dog Joey came upstairs and laid down really close alongside me. I was facing Joey and my tears were falling on his face when the door opened and my Lara walked in and realised by looking at me that Nanny had gone and left us. She cuddled up the other side of Joey and she cried on Joey's head too.

It was the spirit of her sister Olive who came to fetch her. They are together now with their nonstop talking, talking over each other. This seems to be a family trait.

I have had several messages from Nan through other Mediums. With one, it was a large turnout in a hall and mine was the first message. The Medium called out, "This lady is asking for Jeanie, my beautiful Jeanie."

I stood up and said that it was for me, as I had been asking all day in my mind for my Nan to come.

The message I got was, "Jean, get old Bob to fix that dripping tap in the kitchen, it's driving me mad."

Spot on. He spoke just like she did. I thanked him as I joined lots of the audience in laughing.

That is all it can be sometimes: short but sweet.

Naturally, I know my Nan is around me - she is always moving the pictures! But it is good also when she comes through somebody else to say 'Hello'.

My earlier life would have been so different and sadder without her. God bless my little Nan. xx

CHAPTER 9

Becoming a Nurse: the start of the training

In 1966 to be accepted to start your Nurse's training you had to pass an interview and sit a two hour written test. After that there was a six week Pupil Training School (PTS). During the week we were shown and practised practical duties, and each Friday for six weeks we sat an exam. The exam was on both practical work and theory of medicine, and we were assessed also for our communication abilities. If we succeeded at the PTS, we were allowed to continue into the following two years of training. This was split between three hospitals: Hothfield Hospital, which was also where we did the PTS; Willesborough Hospital, a medical hospital in the North side of Ashford; and Ashford Hospital, a surgical hospital in the centre of Ashford.

My training was a great turning point in my life, profoundly changing my ideas and inner thoughts.

During my PTS, I lived in one of the two Nurses' homes on site. It was a Tudor style house called Pine Trees. Miss Taylor, a tall woman with a large bosom, lived there, and all the new student Nurses were in her care for the first six weeks at the start of their training. She appeared stern and strict, but she was a truly sincere person. She loved her pet corgi dog, Rolly, and it went everywhere with her. She also loved her girls, especially if you were kind enough to walk the dog. She would daily impart words of wisdom to these fresh-faced young girls. Miss Taylor liked me. I think she realised that I was a lonely soul, and did try to look after me. I am sure I reflected her own lost sad feelings and for that I shall never forget her.

At the end of our six week PTS, we had to go through a medical examination. This was set up at the Ashford Hospital, in the Nurses' home there. There we all were, waiting in the reception area, wearing only our Bri-Nylon dressing gowns, slippers, and just a pair of knickers on underneath. We were accompanied by the Assistant Matron; it felt like sheep being led to slaughter. Lying on the couch wearing only your knickers was *so* humiliating. I remember the doctor, with his strong-smelling aftershave, even lifted the top of the knicker-band to have a look down.

"Yes, everything is fine," he announced.

And I was thinking, 'And why shouldn't it be?' My God, do you know, not one of us spoke about it. We all stayed quiet in the Nurses' transport bus going back to our own Nurses' home. I suppose we all felt a little bit shocked. Thank goodness, it just wouldn't happen at all now.

After that I started my two year training. I moved

to the other Nurses' Home onsite, Pine Wood, presided over by Miss Horton.

In the sixties things were very strict in the nursing profession, and appearances were very important to being a professional nurse. When I was fourteen, I had had an accident which left me with several chipped teeth: a friend of mine, a terrible flirt, was trying to get this lad's attention by throwing stones in the air at him. Unfortunately for me, one went above my head. The friend, Stella, shouted out my name in warning and I looked up and as I did it came crashing into my mouth. It goes to show that I have had a forgiving nature from an early age, as I remained good friends with her until she died several years ago. I had suffered with my teeth looking like this for four years, in the most impressionable years for a young girl, because I was scared of the local dentist, nicknamed the Butcher. My Mum had ignored the situation. Miss Horton took me aside and said that I would have to go to the dentist and have it fixed, "It is very important to look good as you are going to be a professional person." Thanks to her help and support, I did get them fixed.

Living at Pine Wood wasn't as pleasant as being at Pine Trees. At night we were locked in and only the night Sister had the key. The windows had been set high up in the bedrooms and you had to stand on a chair to look out. The grass outside had been allowed to grow high, and reached the windowsills, almost six feet from the ground. This was all with the aim of keeping men out but six of the other Nurses there habitually smuggled their boyfriends in and kept them there overnight! If there had been a fire, we would probably have been burnt alive. Life was so different then; we just had to accept the conditions or leave.

I had the dubious pleasure of starting at the Geriatric Hospital at Hothfield Hospital, where my Great Grandmother had spent her final days. Everyone had their own nickname for the hospital. I called it Salem's Hospital; the name seemed appropriate because it was a cold and scary place.

The hospital had red bricks at the front of the building, but it still seemed a very dark, dingy and imposing building. The entrance hall had two sets of double doors. Inside to the left were the Porter's Lodge and the Matron's Office. A staircase off to the right went up to the Doctors' quarters. We all got invited to some great parties there. If you were young and pretty, sometimes they turned out to be a little awkward, with young doctors who promised so much if you slept with them. I had a good time just flirting, but they never got anywhere with me.

The doors opposite the double doors led outside onto a large garden area with small grey walls. There were neat edges around the flower beds and in the middle sat a water fountain, trying to give a softer look to the place. Quite often when I had a split shift I would sit on one of the garden's wooden benches to contemplate life.

On our first day we had the pleasure of being introduced to the Matron, whom I had many encounters with during my eight months period there. Later on in the afternoon our group of fourteen students got shown around the place. By the looks on their faces, I was not the only one who was regretting it. My thoughts drifted back to Agnes Rose, having to suffer being put here. It seemed sad to me, not even to be given a choice in the matter of your own life. I cried that night for that poor little old lady who was my Great Grandmother.

One of the matron's upsets with me was my hairstyle: it was far too fashionable. It had been cut in the great Vidal Sassoon style, long one side, short the other. I was always being offered hair clips to hold it back.

"Nurse Wilder, you cannot possibly see clearly," which I couldn't, but I wasn't going to admit that to her.

"Change your hairstyle, for goodness sake."

I would say, "Yes, Matron," but I never did.

Next, my nails were too long so I had to cut them in front of her: just like a child, along with three other girls. There would be uproar if they tried it today. What a sacrifice that was, if only she had known! I had bitten them as a young child and was proud of their length. I was told that her appearance had never changed in all the years she had worked there. Her hair was worn in the typical no nonsense basin cut, she was a plain Jane sort of lady and was never seen to smile or laugh. What a shame to take life so seriously!

We had green and white striped uniform dresses. They had short sleeves with white cuffs. The dresses were much too long, and so we all took the hem up. But it was me again, that was singled out and had to stand by her desk as she unpicked it to lengthen it again. I was tutting to myself, thinking 'Never mind Jeanette, it will go up again tonight.' I must have driven her mad! Although I was a quiet girl I stood my ground.

Another thing that was dreadful about living in the Nurses' home was the lack of privacy. One day after my shift I was given a message from the Ward Sister to go to Matron's Office. This I did, and was quite surprised at her line of questioning.

"I want you to know Nurse Wilder, I have checked your bedroom this morning and it is as I would expect it to be: clean and tidy. But tell me where your belongings are?"

I felt slightly confused and embarrassed by her line of questions. All the time I was thinking, 'She has been in my room! Why are we given a key if anyone else can enter it and look through your private things?'

"Well, Nurse?"

"I don't know what you mean Matron," I replied.

"Your things," she repeated, raising her voice.

I had hung up my other two uniform dresses in the wardrobe and the rest of my clothes were in the white suitcase under my bed. I looked at her, puzzled.

"Oh, haven't you any pictures of your parents, books other than medical ones, soft toys, etc?"

"No, I don't own anything but my white suitcase."

Her second line of questioning to me was:

"Where do you stay when you go home, Nurse?"

"I used to stay with parents of friends until my Grandfather died, now I stay at my Nan's home. I don't go back to the family home as it is too uncomfortable as my brother won't let me be there. Until I had to for a short period, when I became ill and I had nowhere else to go to." A wandering nomad, I suppose that is why I like travelling about.

I did not think about what had happened to my

belongings until she made me think about it. That afternoon I felt a bit down and a slight annoyance at being made to confront it. I hadn't felt that I was a victim until she had gone on about having nothing. I had thought that I was a lucky person in having my Nan's love and the consideration and kindness I had received from people during different periods of my life. The lesson I learnt that day was to remember not to let other people make you feel that way.

Needless to say, I grew up quite quickly. Life seemed so different, training to become a nurse. I saw my first dead person. It is something you never quite come to terms with. Perhaps as you get older you cope better: it's the training and being more professional.

That place felt like a horror movie. The small admission ward housed twenty-two women. The ward above had the same number of men. The other male ward and the three female wards had between thirty to forty patients in each. What a nightmare! All these different people, all coming from different backgrounds. The majority of them never ever had any visitors. They must have felt as if they had been sent to hell. They were in rows, bed after bed. The noise, that's something else I can recall. Those people crying out, shouting and screaming, day and night. It sounded like animals in pain. Looking back, I guess it was probably the worst place that I could have gone to, being a sensitive person and psychic. Although I do believe it helped me to become a more compassionate person and have feelings for a complete stranger's miseries.

Working on night duty did seem very scary for all of us young women. It was so isolated and surrounded by woodland. There is a village a few miles away called Hothfield, and this is near the huge common heath. About ten minutes walk away from the main hospital there was a lake with a hut styled building at the side of it. This was another ward. We had to walk there unless the weather turned nasty; the senior staff rode down in comfort. Unfortunately, trainee nurses came far down in the pecking order.

Usually around eight patients were sent there to convalesce and there were two permanent patients that stayed there until they passed away. So only two staff were needed to work each shift. The Night Sister or the Charge Nurse would arrive to check over all that had to be done, and to administer the drugs, as I was not a trained nurse yet. They arrived around nine o'clock and then were not seen or heard of again until seven in the morning. I experienced something awful in that place.

I can remember it all so clearly to this day. I was on duty with a lovely mature lady called Ivy. I suppose she was only in her middle thirties, but when you are eighteen that does seem old. She was quite plump, with brown eyes and dark short hair, but had a lovely face with a clear complexion. She usually wore a look on her face that said 'Do not mess with me!' I got on well with her, but if your face did not fit with her, well, oh dear! We set off together at half past seven: the shift started at seven forty-five pm.

This particular March night it felt so cold and frosty that we persuaded the porter to give us a ride in his car. He fancied Ivy, so he agreed. It only took a few minutes, not long, letting him be back in his lodge before anyone had noticed. The two day staff handed us the report about our ten patients: nothing too serious.

All the patients were men. Nice old boys. If they wanted a cup of tea in the night and a chat they got it; their stories about their lives never failed to surprise me. And so it was general nursing care, plus the important dressings on Mr Pringer's legs, plus bedsores. All but one of them were incontinent so it was heavy work. We had our routine and went about our duty.

The security was the first job, to check that all the windows and doors were shut and locked up. Second was making of the hot drinks - the medicines had been given to the patients earlier. Then we began the first of the few rounds that took place during the night.

Mr Pringer had MS, (multiple sclerosis), and was hard to handle at times because of his rigid limbs, and so we left him to last, as he took us a lot longer than the others. This gave the other men time to settle and go to sleep. My build was slight but I could always lift well. I updated the report before sitting down. Come eleven thirty, we were ready to have our sandwiches and a cup of tea. After doing another ward check we settled down for an hour or longer, unless anyone called us. The place felt so eerie that we kept in sight of each other most of the night. Although officially no member of staff is supposed to sleep on night duty everyone did when they could. After another round at 2am we settled down again in the comfy armchairs. What happened next was unbelievable. We fell asleep quite quickly and I was dreaming that Mr Pringer was chasing me. He was acting like someone demented with a knife in his hand. I know that I was shouting, and with my eyes open I looked straight at Ivy saying, "Wake me up!"

But nothing was coming out. Ivy was frozen to the chair, staring back at me, with her mouth open as if she was screaming. We had to force ourselves to wake up.

I said, "What has happened to us?" We both had had the same nightmare. The air felt strange and cold. Ivy was a very strong minded and down to earth person, but her 'nothing frightens me' attitude was falling apart. We both went icy cold; when people say the hairs on the back of your neck stand up, it's true. Ivy jumped up and slammed the office door shut. I went into a nervous laugh, until she said, "Shut up!" which I promptly did.

How do two people have the same nightmare together? "What was making that loud noise?" we both said, staring at one another.

"It sounded like someone walking, Ivy".

"I know," she said, "but none of them can walk. Do you think somebody's broken in?"

My reply was, "I'm sure we would have heard it earlier." Inside, I was about to scream and hang off the ceiling. I was telling myself, you have always been able to keep in control in difficult situations, but who was I kidding? Panic was setting in.

"Let's ring the porter, and ask him to come and check the place over."

"Alright, OK, we'll do that."

So we agreed and got onto the porter. He said he

would finish the job he was currently doing and then come down before the next, which was taking a patient who had died to the mortuary.

His cheerful voice came down the telephone, "I'll be with you around twenty minutes, alright?"

I wanted to bellow, 'Thank you, we'll all be dead, take your time' but didn't. Turning to Ivy I said, "We've got to check the patients are all safe."

Ivy replied, "Nobody is calling out, they must be asleep. Let's have a cup of tea to calm our nerves."

So we did, and afterwards the porter had still not arrived. It was a joint decision that we must go and look around. We opened the office door as quietly as we could, with our two heads poking round the door.

I said doubtfully, "It seems OK?"

Opposite the office was a broom cupboard. Armed with a broom each, we ventured out into the corridor, Ivy in front, as I had slipped behind her saying, "You're the eldest." With the dim night lights throwing odd shadows off the walls, we were so highly strung that if anyone had come around that corner then, the pair of us would have been looking at life in prison. The newspaper headlines: 'Two nurses on night duty went crazy and thrashed man to death with brooms'.

The second room was where the medicines were kept. Further down on the left was the ward where all seemed quiet. On we went towards the lounge which was at the far end of the corridor of the long hut. This room spread across the width of the hut. There was an almighty bang.

"God in heaven!" Ivy screamed, "What the hell was that?"

We leapt into the air. By now we were terrified, but trying to be brave. We swung the door open, and Ivy's hand slid into the darkness of the room to the right and switched the lights on. Then we peered into the room: nothing, except that the small window at the back of the room was wide open. How could that be? We had checked the security together: it was definitely locked.

The window had been opened from the inside. We shut it and then went around the rest of the place to make sure that we were safe. "Right, let's look in at the men." With my hand on the door handle, just ready to turn the knob, we heard talking coming from inside the room. It sounded like a clear voice. Who could it be? We walked slowly into the room; they were all asleep. I grabbed Ivy's arm, "Mr Pringer." We crept in closer and closer towards the bed.

He was having a conversation with someone. It couldn't be. He was speaking clearly, and we knew that was not possible. MS affects the nervous system, which causes defects in speech pronunciation. He was still asleep, and then his eyes opened, staring straight pass us, and he shouted out, "HAS SHE GONE?" Then he closed his eyes and went back to sleep.

We stood staring at one another. Now the other men were disturbed and restless, so we pulled ourselves together and got on and did another ward round.

At that age I wasn't into drinking, but I would not have said no to a large brandy, for medicinal purposes!

The porter then arrived, and had a good look around the building, inside and out. He sat himself down into a big old leather armchair, and I made him a cup of coffee.

"Well, you girls got spooked then," he laughed out loud. "Not like you, Ivy." We had told him that we had heard noises.

Ivy tentatively asked, "Who died then, Harry?"

"Mrs Pringer, the wife of the old guy down here."

We gave each other a glance, and I was beginning to feel quite faint. It was all starting to be too much for my nerves as I was still only eighteen and half. But we never said anything in front of the porter. The time we had our nightmare was an hour after she had died, when they say the spirit leaves the body. The old lady had visited her husband before she had departed from this world.

The porter told us something about the history of their marriage. The porter's wife had grown up a few doors up from them in one of the local villages so knew them quite well. The marriage had been very volatile: she threw things, and it was said he threatened her with a knife, chased her out of their house and into the street. You know when you are watching a thriller on the television or at the pictures, when the music gets loud and dramatic? Well that's what it felt like, the drums were rolling in my head like somebody, or something was about to leap out at me. Ivy and I stared at each other with wide eyes and fixed looks on our faces.

When we left at quarter to eight in the morning, to walk back up the lane we felt heavy footed and weary, and both of us looked a little pale.

I turned to Ivy, "That was a bit much."

"Yes, yes it was," she said, "I need to get home. I'm tired out."

We kept it our secret - how on earth could we have told anyone? We both realised we shared the gift of being psychic, but people did not discuss such things back then in 1967 in case you were thought of as a nutcase. I really wanted to be a trained Nurse, and it certainly would not have helped my career.

I have been with many people when they depart from this world. It can be like a soft breeze passing, sometimes touching you as it goes. Some curtains around a bed can gently move. Many times just nothing is heard, and it is so quiet and peaceful. A few people that pass on as angry souls leave this world as Mrs Pringer did. Some fight refusing to believe that their time to go is near.

CHAPTER 10

Return to Salem's: juggling married life and work

I met the man I would marry when I was seventeen, but I did not want to go out with him. I had other boyfriends and then, when was I was nineteen, I was out with some friends and met Bob again; his sense of humour won me over. Much later he told me that I just took his breath away. We were engaged after six months and married at the age of twenty. That was that! Before we got married my Mum asked me if I was sure. "I will love him till I die," I replied.

After my training finished I worked at Ashford Hospital for a while, until I was pregnant with Luke. I was working on a men's surgical ward and the Sister expected me to keep lifting heavy men when I was six months gone. One day, a porter intervened, "Sister, you can't expect that Nurse to lift that man!" She did though, so I moved to a private ward which was lighter work.

On to October 1970. The year was nearly ending and I had decided to go back to work at the hospital. My baby was ten months old, and we needed the extra money. My husband was working up in London at that time, spending long hours travelling back and forth. I asked a friend's mother if she could have Luke for me during the nights that I worked, as my husband left at 6am in morning: it would be impossible for me to get back home before he had left. She agreed and I started back doing three shifts of night duty a week. Looking back with hindsight, it was one of the first major bad decisions I have made, and unfortunately I've made a few. Being young and happily married, and with our young baby, I see now that I took on too much.

I had to organise everything for Luke. Feed, bath him and put all the necessary things together in his pram that he would want for the night, and also for the next morning. Plus sort out the extra freshly made bottles that Delia would need to give him. I felt happy to leave Luke with Delia as she was a very kind and caring lady and was also a retired trained nurse. This worked quite well for a year and then one day Luke came home with his knitted jacket half-eaten by Delia's large black poodle Peppy. Then I had to rethink the situation! He was a happy soul, always laughing, and such a pretty baby. People often mistook him for a girl.

After a while I gradually felt so tired and run down. The routine of taking care of a baby, doing the housework, and making sure that my husband's meal was ready in the oven for him for when he came home from work was a lot to cope with. Years ago very few men helped with any housework; it just wasn't expected. The shopping I did on my own with a baby in tow just wasn't easy. I also used to care for my dear little Nan, and try to help my Dad as well. I helped Nan with washing and ironing her curtains, and with mowing her lawn until she got a gardener. I took care of her hands and feet, and did the washing and cutting of her hair until we arranged for a local chap from a nearby hair salon to come. I organised her calls for home visits with the district nurse and the doctor.

As I lived on the opposite side of Ashford to where my Nan and Dad lived it made life very difficult at times. I did not drive then and using public transport was just as bad in the seventies as it is now. Maybe perhaps not quite as many people pushing and shoving to get on the buses as there are now. I'd get a phone call from Nan, would I get her some vests on 'Appro' - you could take things home from some shops then, 'on approval'. They would write out a ticket and the person would pay for them later if they wanted to keep the vests or other pieces of clothing, for example, shoes or slippers. On occasions my Nan could be very naughty. Back and forth I would have to go.

"Oh, I have changed my mind."

"Mmmm, OK," I would mutter. Sometimes I felt I wanted to strangle her; she had no idea about time, distance, or my routine of life with a husband, baby, housework and the responsibility of work. Really, it would just be an excuse to get me to visit her. Never mind, I did love her; I was just overwhelmed.

By Christmas I was feeling exhausted and I caught the flu. My health seemed to go downhill after that. I developed bronchitis and then the allergies kicked in and then followed the awful years having bronchial asthma.

Back to Salem's. I would drop off Luke and run up to the main road, Faversham Road, to get a bus to the town to catch the 7.15pm transport in the town which took us out of town to the hospital to start the night shift at 7.45pm until 7.45 am. They were a good bunch of women and two chaps that I worked with.

The Sister on night duty was a small, rounded, Scottish woman who talked extremely fast and with a strong Glaswegian accent. I was always heard to be saying, "What did she say?" She would demand, "Are you deaf, Nurse?" She was married but they had no children. Thank goodness, for she was a bully and had very little patience for anything or anybody. Unfortunately for us she had no sense of humour either. She was strict, had a fierce tone and never smiled once in three years that I knew her, the old bat.

It was impossible to attend to all the patients before ten o'clock lights out. We continued working with the dimmer lights on until the last patient was settled for the night. As I was a trained nurse, I did the medicine round. And sometimes it was as late as midnight and the poor old people were fast asleep when we would wake them up and say, "Here is your sleeping tablet." It had to be done! If they did not get them they would be wide awake from 2am causing all sorts of problems. For two staff, nursing up to forty patients was a big responsibility.

During the night I would go off and sort out the medicines, and then put them into pots labelled with the names of the patients on a tray for the morning. Then there was the worry what if you dropped them or knocked over the tray, it would be a mass of mixed tablets. The very thought made me have my nervous giggle. Everybody had to do it this way, as there wasn't time in the morning.

I was working up on the first floor which was a women's ward. On a Wednesday night I was on my own. This is not allowed now. There has to be two of you, checking, adding up the remaining tablets that are left in the bottles and then signing in a book. I was doing the medicines and I felt this creepy sensation of being watched go right through me. The hairs on the back of my neck felt as if they were all standing up on end. The place was pretty gloomy with a sallow yellow look due to the old lighting and very old dark creamy yellow paint. I started talking to myself, "Oh, God!" I prayed, telling myself to stay calm and finish what I was doing. And so I did, and then I panicked when I looked behind me and saw a bright orange ball floating about three feet above me in the air. I did not know at the time that spirits sometimes appear as orbs. Oh dear! I screamed like a demented woman and ran like a lunatic. The noise must have been deafening below as we used to have to wear quite heavy black shoes as part of our uniform. In my flight to get away I tripped on one of the corners of a bed and went hurtling through the air: I fell flat on my face and the keys went flying. Laying there groaning, I had realised I had woken most of the patients. It sounded like being in the zoo. The staff from across the landing, another women's ward, arrived to see what all the fuss was about. Two staff from below our ward also stood before me. "Healey, what the hell happened?" With help I picked myself up off the floor. I went on to explain myself, and asked if anybody else had ever seen the floating orange ball. "No," they replied, staring straight at me. Muttering, they went back to their own wards.

Feeling pretty stupid I went into the ward's office to start some of the reports on the patients. I was quietly sitting at the desk when the night Sister called Mavis, who was in charge, came in. She stood behind me asking me was I alright. "Yes, I am fine, thank you," I replied. Then she did something very odd by putting her hands in my hair saying, "Haven't you got lovely hair, Jeanette." I was taken aback and felt uncomfortable. At that moment the care helper, Pauline, from the ward below us came in and sat beside me. Mavis left. In a whisper, Pauline mouthed to me, "Mavis is a lesbian. Be careful, she obviously likes you." I was dismayed: she knew I was married so why was she coming on to me? These days I would have reported the incident of her unwanted attention.

It was Pauline's break and handing me a cup of coffee, she whispered, "I've seen it." I turned to look at her. "Have you? That's good as I thought that I was going mad!" She told me that she was psychic and looking me straight in the eyes said, "So are you." Looking back at her I nodded.

She went on to say "There are children's spirits that have gone over and they are trying to contact you."

"Why me?"

"They know that you will listen to them, Jeanette." Later on children were to play a role in my psychic world, in odd ways. The feelings I had were mixed: nervous but I felt relieved. I was to experience similar things years later when I was working in the Residential Home at Ashford.

It felt like being part of a small, elite group who were frightened to say too much, for fear of being branded weirdos.

After that incident, when we were on the same shift, Pauline and I would share our break time together, telling each other stories.

One particular Monday night it was blowing a gale until 3am in the morning and then the winds began to drop slightly. Being such an old building everything rattled and shook. The large, old fashioned, sash windows, with divided small panes, fitted poorly and the curtains would blow around with the draught. Also, the curtains did not always meet in the middle and so the patients could see the lightning flashing across the sky and it was not nice at all for them. Some would be whimpering with fear. The Sister did her rounds early that evening to get back to her cosy room and have two or three drinks. And we are not talking tea or coffee here!

That night we had a very poorly lady who was dying. I was in charge and had to deal with the laying out of the body when she did die and take care of sorting through her personal affects.

The Doctor who was on the duty list had to be called out to pronounce the death and to leave a death certificate. This was the Sister's job. She also had to phone any listed relatives to relay the information of the death. Some of the patients had nobody at all, so sad.

The poor lady did die during the night. The Sister wasn't happy at having to deal with it, acting as though it was most inconvenient that she had died before 8am and not after her shift had finished. Still, she duly phoned the Doctor who came within half an hour and signed the death certificate.

After I had completed the laying out I rang the porter who was in the porter's lodge and asked if he could come to collect the deceased person. We would together put her into the small mortuary which was situated along side of the main laundry building. The mortuary was facing the lake and unprotected from the weather. Gordon, an overweight man in his thirties, was not keen to go out, "She is going to have to wait until the rain eases off. We would be drenched as soon as we stepped outside. She's not in any hurry, is she?" He was right.

There were only three of us, myself, Pauline and Shirley, looking after fifty patients that night. We were down one member of staff: Christine, a trained nurse, rang in too late to get a replacement and so we had to make do. I was the only trained Nurse but I knew that I had two good care assistants on with me. They knew what had to be done, and so we worked well together and got on with it. After we had finished our work routine, when it was cold like this, the staff would wrap themselves up in a white sheet to keep warm sitting in the large armchairs. We took a break to have a sandwich and a hot cup of packet soup as all seemed quiet on the western front. We snuggled into our sheets in some comfy chairs with our feet up on the walls: we were frightened of creepy crawlies on the floor in the dark, especially cockroaches. That's what we always did, all facing the wall because we were always frightened something would get us.

We were in a large sitting room area between the two wards. The kitchen was on the other side of the twenty bed ward and so when we wanted a drink we had to sneak back and forth because we didn't want to disturb any of the patients.

It was very quiet with not a sound indoors or out; it seemed almost as if everyone had stopped breathing, and the quiet deepened into an unearthly silence.

We whispered to each other and agreed that it didn't seem natural at all. All of a sudden, brisk footsteps broke the silence. "Oh, my goodness, it's the old dragon; we're in for it now!" The footsteps came right into the middle of the room, a few feet away from our backs and then stopped, turned and went out again. We were all peering over the top of our sheets at one another like children.

Staring at each other, the air was icy and our breath could be seen in front of us, a slight breeze blew past the backs of the chairs. "I thought it was her, the Sister," Shirley said with some relief in her voice. If it had been the dragon then the three of us would have had to go to the Matron's office in the morning, to be reprimanded.

"No," I told them, "it must have been Lily's spirit leaving her body. Perhaps she used to walk briskly when she was young?" Then the air changed and the normal sounds at night could be heard again.

Next, came an almighty bang on the main outside door: it was Gordon, "Come on then, let me in, you girls." We all jumped up out of our chairs together, I am sure that we all suffered heart palpitations. Everything was ready, and so I took Lily on her last journey, hopefully, I thought to myself, on to a better place in the next world to meet up with friends and loved ones. When I returned to the ward the Sister was waiting for me. "Did you remove her wedding ring?" she barked at me, "The relatives want it." Why hadn't she told me this earlier? Seething internally, I knew that I had to go back. It was bad enough the first time but going back into that place a second time, well, my skin was already crawling at the thought.

There had been another death just before the night duty had begun that night. That made two bodies in the small mortuary and Gordon hated it as much as I did, almost spitting out, "The old cow did it on purpose," referring to the Sister, "That one has an evil streak in her." He was right. We were outside again, and I pulled my cloak tightly around me. Nurses were issued with dark green cloaks with red linings back then, they were smart and warm.

It was raining hard again, and so we were getting whipped about by the wind and the rain. Going past the lake was an ordeal in itself; Gordon was shouting, "Watch out for monsters dragging their wretched bodies up from the depth!" Laughing, he said, "Come on!" He unlocked the door for the second time this night and switched the dim light on. Stepping back he pushed me in through the door first. We pulled back the sheet and I took her left hand in mine, but rigor mortis had started to set in.

"Gordon, you will have to help me to pull it off."

Between us we managed to prise the ring off, but to my dismay as we were doing it there was a cracking sound.

"Gordon, you broke her finger!"

He pulled a rueful face, "I didn't mean to. Look, if we hadn't retrieved it, old Walker would have sent us right back again."

It still felt like robbing from the dead. I said sorry and goodbye to Lily.

As we turned to go out there was a shuffling sound from the corner of the room. Gordon, for his all his bravado, grabbed my hand and we ran for the door. I dropped the ring, and outside standing in the rain we had a debate as to who would go back in.

"Let's calm down, it had to be rats."

So we squeezed through the door together and Gordon leaned down and snatched up the ring and we ran back slamming the door behind us as we hastily left. That was a true act of bravery on Gordon's part as he was a coward and didn't mind admitting it.

What a night!

I never told my husband any of this as he wouldn't have let me go back there. We were young and in love. He would now; it would be "Off you go as we need the money!" And laugh.

After a couple of years, I fell pregnant with my lovely daughter Lara and left work. I didn't go back to work until Lara started school: not only did I have two young children, and Nan and Dad, but the bronchial asthma was causing me real problems.

A few days after our daughter was born I had a bad asthma attack and so had to remain in hospital longer. Then when she was a couple of weeks old I had a slight breathless attack during the night. I felt better in the morning so my husband left for work.

Gradually I got washed and dressed and did the same for Luke who was almost four. Lara was a quiet baby and I lifted her out of the crib and laid her on the bed and changed her nappy. I started feeling unwell and breathless and sat down on the bed. Then it went into a full blown asthma attack which really frightened me. Luke was wide eyed and started to softly cry, "Mummy, Mummy."

I glanced over at the mirror and I could see my lips had gone blue.

"It's alright darling, Mummy will be alright. Just help Mummy please."

So I struggled and picked Lara up and put her under my left arm. Luke followed me to the top of the stairs. I leaned against the balusters and got Luke to sit on the top step of the stairs. Then I put Lara on his lap and asked him to hold her tight so she didn't fall down the stairs.

Step by step I slowly climbed down, taking Lara and putting her under my left arm again with Luke following and helping me hold her. At the bottom I sat on the bottom step and Luke started patting my head, "Alright Mummy, alright Mummy." He must have been so frightened, poor little boy.

I could not stand up again and so I got on my hands and knees with Lara tucked under my arm again and crawled along the hall. It had taken so long and Lara was whimpering now.

Then I asked Luke to sit on the floor and put Lara across his knees whilst I gripped at things to pull myself up to the sink. I could not feed her myself and had to make her a bottle; how I did it I don't know. Then I gave the bottle to Luke and talking through gasps of air told him to hold her head up and try and see if she would drink it.

My two little babies sat on the floor: she sucked and drank some milk as he said, "There, there," to her, mimicking what he had heard me say to her. I gave him milk in a cup and biscuits because they were the only things at hand on the work surface in the kitchen.

It was ages until I felt I could crawl back down the hall again with Lara under my arm to try and phone the Doctor. He came almost immediately, leaving the Surgery full of people.

When he entered through the front door he was greeted with the sight of me looking slightly grey in colour, with pinched cheeks and blue lips. My Luke was clinging to my leg and Lara was lying close to me on the stairs. He quickly gave me an injection and rang for an ambulance. Then he lifted Lara and took her to the dining room and put her in the carrycot, saying, "What a beautiful baby!"

When the ambulance arrived I was put on oxygen and given another injection as I was light headed and feeling faint. I was helped into the sitting room, and they tried to give words of comfort to Luke. But he wasn't having any of it and was still attached tightly to my leg! The paramedic made up another two bottles for me to give to Lara and he changed her nappy. I refused to go into hospital as I was adamant I wasn't leaving my babies! Luckily, my lovely neighbour Nora had came home from work and came in to see what was happening. She agreed to keep an eye on me until my husband arrived home from work. Nora fed Luke and put something aside for Bob for his supper. Dr Bush came back later in the evening to administer more medication and had a word with Bob and said I could have died. He came back the next day also. In fact this incident really changed my life as it was the start of me taking steroids, which helped my breathing but upset my weight.

Still, I survived the attack and had many more over the years. Notably when Luke was about 14: he and Lara came in from school and again I was stuck upstairs fighting for breath. I could hear Luke shouting down the phone "Get here quick my Mum is having a heart attack!" We laughed about it afterwards. He said, "The stupid Receptionist was telling me they were too busy and that you cannot die from asthma, so I told her that my Mum was having a heart attack as well!" Such a good son.

I have so much empathy for others who struggle to breath. Anybody who suffers the affects of long term illness struggles to maintain a normal lifestyle. Thankfully, after I got my own nebuliser it became easier to cope.

Anyway, one summer, when Lara was about eight months old, I worked with a few of the local ladies on the farms around Ashford picking strawberries, gooseberries and apples. I took both of the children with me, which was a handful. It was hard work and I didn't earn much money because I kept stopping to check what Luke was up to or to comfort Lara if she was crying. The other women thought I was a bit posh as I always look so nice. I wore white cotton trousers which I washed every night; I must have been mad! We had a few laughs together though.

Then in 1978, Lara started school and I went back to work at the residential home, Kennington Place. I worked there for eleven years. Later, I decided to go back again to Salem's as a relief nurse. I only lasted two nights, it was awful. The first night I was there my close friend Elaine was on duty. She had gone there when Kennington Place had closed down. She showed me the ropes. The second night I was in charge and I just could not cope. I was handed a huge bunch of keys and left to get on with it. It was too much responsibility as I had not been up-dated with all the medicines, and I felt that I could have just sat down and cried. Again, it felt unwelcoming and spooky. I knew that I could not do this, not this time around. Dear Elaine and Lynne continued working there for some time after. Poor Elaine had had a hard path to walk, bringing up three boys and having a husband who was a long-term invalid. She kept her sense of humour throughout all the years and did a wonderful job. Her boys are a real credit to her.

Elaine was a wonderful friend to me and also to Lynne, and she always recommended us for nursing positions when we needed jobs.

I went back to take some photos of the place in December 2002. Wandering around outside I had the strangest feeling: that odd sensation you get, when going back to your past and reliving it again.

The long hut at the lakeside where we had nursed patients and the Nurses' home, Pine Wood, were now derelict. The long grass that had surrounded the home was gone.

The fountain is still in the front garden, but the laundry rooms and the mortuary have gone, along with the kitchens and large staff dining room that was used as a teaching room in the afternoons.

I took several photos but the one that I should have taken, I did not as it happened too quickly, and I was shocked and surprised. As I was walking around to the back of the main building something made me stop and look up at one of the rear bedroom windows: there was a face at the window. It all happened too quickly for me to respond. I cannot even be sure if it was a male or female that was staring back. It was someone that had a small head and appeared to be very thin. It faded before me, just like I was seeing a ghost. I later asked the nurse in the reception area if she know who it was. Her reply was, "You must have seen a ghost. There aren't any bedrooms along that end, just a corridor. Also they would have to be at least seven foot in height as the windows are high up!" If only I had been quicker, who knows what I might have caught on film?

I continued towards the lake and standing and staring across it, it still had an uneasiness to it that I cannot explain. I turned and walked along the left side of the lake towards the empty remains of the Nursing Hut, Lakeside. I took more photos and picked teasels, thinking of my home. They would look nice in my long vase that stood in the kitchen in the alcove where a fire once had stood in our one hundred year old cottage that we were renting.

All of it has gone now, they are going to build on that piece of land and also down by the lake. Let's hope whoever lives, or stays there, does not get too many disturbed nights!

I would not live there now for love or any amount of money!

Good luck to all who reside there...................

CHAPTER 11

The Residential Home: Kennington Place

This was another strange period in my life. Good and bad!

I applied to be a night care assistant at the local home, because my second child, our daughter Lara, was ready to start school. It was just down the road from where we lived, for two nights a week: a Saturday and Sunday one week, a Wednesday and a Thursday night the following. So, I was back to working and running a home. It was a lot to juggle: the family to look after, the dreaded shopping and cooking, my Nan and Dad needed help as well, and we had a dog, called Joey.

Where did the saying come from.........Super Mum? Let's be honest that has always applied to working Mums! Anyway the job suited me as the hours were 9.30pm until 7.30am which fitted into the family time. My husband still worked long days, quite often coming home as late as 9pm.

The Residential Home housed around forty residents and was run extremely well. It was still the policy there that the residents came first. The Home was a large, J-shaped, two story building, with a garden surrounding it and two large greenhouses. This was set in a housing area. It was run by a Superintendent and his wife, the Matron, for the local council. In the following years when society changed we had to call them by their first names. This took some getting used to! I found it difficult as I had been used to calling superiors (as we thought of our bosses then!) by their surname or the title that they had earned. This comes from my training and is old fashioned now. My dear friend Elaine was working there and put my name forward for the job. Elaine worked with Sue on the Monday and Tuesday nights every week. Two other ladies worked the alternate nights to us; they were a nice team of work mates. My colleague was a lovely lady, a little older than me. She had a much laid back personality; her name was Pat, and we got on very well. We ended up working together for eight years and became very good friends. Pat was one of the Matron's younger sisters. As we got to know each other we found that we seemed to trigger off many psychic situations at work. I believe that the psychic energy between us opened up the channels for the spirits to come through.

They were lucky to have us and a few other women who were trained nurses, but we were employed as care assistants, which meant lower wages for experienced staff.

I can tell you this: it was such gruelling hard work!

When we left in the mornings we felt completely exhausted. The routine started at 9.30pm with the report and then we had to set the trolley up and offer a hot drink and give the medicines to the residents. Then next was the night round to settle the residents down and made sure that they were made comfortable for the night, changing any wet beds and helping anyone who needed it onto the commodes.

There were four large sitting rooms to clean, hoovering and polishing, or wet dusting, and wiping the blinds. There were two large toilets to clean downstairs, then hoovering and polishing the office. We had to put on the two washing machines and in some cases doing the laundry continued throughout the night. The clean washing was hung in the airing room and removed when dry, before the morning staff came on duty. Also, we were expected to do the ironing of clothes for the residents. Just remember, we had forty residents to look after and some that were up watching the television had to be undressed and put to bed and the same applied in getting them up the next morning! Then there were the cups of tea made if anyone wanted one during the night, if they were unable to sleep. In the dining room, the cloths which covered over the plates and cutlery for the night had to be removed from the tables in the morning. The bread and butter had to be done during the early morning and wrapped up in wet muslin to keep it moist for breakfast. There was the filling and removing anything left in the dishwasher, cleaning the kitchen, and tidying the sluice. The hardest part was all the nursing care. God, that was a mouthful and I could go on, but I am sure by now you have the picture. Oh yes, we were such martyrs, but a lot was expected from the night staff. Health and safety regulations would not permit it now.

But we did have many moments of laughter and fun. One particular night we arrived for night duty and were greeted by an Assistant Matron from the Dover Agency. She had been booked for two nights sleep-in. I will call her Gill. She was very thin with lots of blonde hair and a high squeaky voice. It was the end of a pleasant warm day and it still felt warm in the air. Gill introduced herself and gave us the fastest report ever given. "Goodnight ladies," as she quickly disappeared into the staff flat, which comprised of four rooms, "see you in the morning." We said to each other that we hoped that there wouldn't be any reason to call her. Our hopes were soon dashed! There was a lot of commotion going on the top landing, and we ran up the stairs to be confronted with a resident screaming, "The Germans are coming!" Her name was June. She was knocking on the other bedroom doors disturbing everybody. Tentatively approaching poor June, we were talking softly and trying to convince her that it was not true. "Help me!" she started yelling at the top of her voice. People were crying and moaning that they wanted to escape or go to sleep. Pat left me to go and knock Gill up, after three or four hard knocks she appeared.

"What is going on? What do you want?"

Pat said "Your assistance, please." After what seemed an eternity they came upstairs together and what a fright Gill did look! She had stopped to back comb and spray her hair, even taking the time applying some lipstick. So there she stood, "Stand aside, I can deal with this."

She was absolutely useless! Instead of calming the situation down she made it ten times worse, saying, "Quick! Run into your rooms and hide! Get into your beds - they won't find you there!" There was absolute uproar. As for June, panic showed in her eyes and she lunged at Gill and grabbed her around the throat. The woman was being throttled; she looked like a Barbie doll in a pink chiffon night dress and dressing gown. I was beside myself with laughter with tears pouring down my face. As Pat pushed me aside she was also laughing, trying to prise June's hands from Gill's throat. Poor Gill was in shock. We took Gill aside and said that June needed to be given something to calm her down. Her reply was, "I don't know what to give her." We suggested that she rang the Doctor on our list, to help give June some medication.

Next she said, "Would one of you do it?" I rang Doctor Williams. He arrived twenty minutes later. Sedation, by way of injection of Valium, was administered, and things started to settle. He came into the staff room with us and sat down and had a cup of tea.

In the meantime, most of our time was taken up with a weeping Gill. "I don't understand it," she wailed, "I have a degree in Psychology. I am usually very good with people." I had laughed when I had rang the doctor; I laughed as I helped put the residents to bed; I laughed as the doctor gave Gill the same sedation as June. I said, "Go back to bed, Gill."

As we put her to bed and tucked her in and promised not to disturb her again Pat and I shook our heads smiling at one another thinking, 'Isn't this your job and isn't that why you get paid more than we do - to be making the right decisions in what should be done?'

The Doctor said, "She is a loony! Why is she in this job?"

At 7.30am the next morning, as we were giving the report about the night's chaos, one of the day care assistants confessed that she had joked with June before she put her to bed that if she did not behave herself the Germans would get her............Oh, dear me!

That said it all, poor June.

That particular Care Assistant was in the habit of being a bit mouthy and putting her foot in it. There was a lady called Madge who was very religious, with her statues and praying everyday in her bedroom. Poor little Madge was crippled with arthritis. Every time as she moved her bones creaked very loudly. One fated morning Penny was helping Madge get dressed. Madge held up a bottle to Penny suggesting that she had some of the contents. "Don't mind if I do," Penny said, and with a big gulp she downed most of the fluid. Poor Madge shouted, "It's my holy water you have drunk! You were supposed to dab a bit on yourself you foolish woman!"

Penny raced from the room, red faced and crying, screaming, "I've been poisoned!" I think everybody had a good laugh at her expense. Penny's penance was to go and get her some more holy water. I believe she was a little quieter for a few days. Divine payback perhaps for what she had done to June!

Mrs Smith had a bad ulcer on her right leg and so we were extra attentive towards her during the night. That dear old lady rang eleven times, and we were there, giving her little chats with her cups of tea and painkillers. Helped her out of bed to use the commode and then, when she did nothing, smiled sweetly at her. We did not have the time to waste as there were other residents that were poorly as well but she needed our attention and got it. Anyway, in we went with our big smiles and the last cup of tea before the morning round, "And how are you this morning?" Mrs Smith replied, "It's good to see you nurses on, you are so lovely, not like those other two last night. They were real bitches to me last night!"

I was speechless; Pat said to me, "Let's go, or I will smother the old cow."

Of all the Christmas Eves and Christmas nights we worked, this could be classed as one of the worst of many.

Ms Emily Tyler was such a sweet lady in her early eighties. She had been a teacher at a girl's school. We found her really interesting to talk to and I know that she enjoyed talking with us over cups of tea. This evening we arrived for night duty to be told that she had been put into sick bay opposite the sluices. Apparently she had a urine infection, which can make the body temperature rise. Antibiotics had been prescribed by the Doctor, who had been called out. When we were on the last drinks round that evening, we entered her room to find her muttering to herself.

Leaning towards her I said, "Emily, how are you feeling, and how about a nice cold drink then?"

"Hello girls," she said, "Who do those children belong to?"

We looked at her and then around the room.

"What children?"

"Oh, they have gone now. They must be having fun with you; they were coughing like Jeanette's asthmatic cough, not Pat's smoker's cough."

Outside, we said she must be hallucinating, and we had better keep an extra eye on her tonight. We continued around the home, distributing drinks and medicines on the way. The last room was Mrs Huston's room, as we walked in, she said, "Whose children are they?"

"What children?" we said together.

"They have gone now. What is the matter with me, am I seeing things?"

Trying to sound nonchalant, "How many children?"

"Three," was her reply, "one boy and two girls."

Mrs Houston was compos mentis and so who were the children that she had seen?

Throughout my life I have had spirit children around me; it's obvious now that they felt they could communicate through me. Because I felt the need to know if this was true or not, I went to a well known respected psychic called Linda for a reading.

We knew each other and the respect was mutual.

She asked me to cut the Tarot cards and then proceeded to give me a reading about what or who was around me. Afterwards we sat opposite one another and held hands. Without any warning she started crying, "How do you deal with all this misery, Jeanette? All these children are around you."

I replied, "Yes, I know."

She went on to describe them, "I see a fairground," and then continued with certain things surrounding it.

She was describing little Lesley-Ann, one of the Moors victims that Ian Brady and Myra Hindley murdered in the 1960s. I never believed that woman had ever changed, and I don't care about either of them. I hope that they both eventually meet up in Hell.

Sometimes even now the other child Keith comes to me, "Come and find me."

I have looked for him at Saddleworth Moor but could not get a connection with the Police at that time. I had been taken seriously though by a journalist from the area and he gave me an Inspector's name to email, but to no avail as there have been too many time wasters.

But back to the story about the Residential Home, the evening was Christmas Eve. We heard funny whisperings as well as light footsteps throughout the night. We did not have time to sit and ponder over this as we had a lady called Mary, who looked like a tiny bird, talking into the handrail on the walls. "Can you hear me?" she yelled. Mary thought she was on the telephone. My nervous giggling didn't help much; she might have been tiny but we had an awful job trying to prise her hands off the handrail and back into her bed. As soon as our backs were turned, she was out of bed again. Another resident, Charlie, screamed all night for his mother. First of all he fell out of bed, this happened twice and lucky for him he did not hurt himself. Then we decided to lug the mattress off the bed and lay him on this. As soon as we were down the corridor there was a terrible crash and more screaming. We raced back to his room and there he was: he had knocked over the side table, clutter everywhere. He had rolled off the mattress and got stuck with his left foot wedged under the radiator on the wall. "Oh, for goodness sake, what are we going to do with him?" Our next idea was to get a wheel chair and bring him downstairs to one of the sitting rooms by the lift. Pat stayed with him in the lift as I went down the stairs. We put him in a big armchair, but he then fell out of it, still screaming, "MOTHER!" Nothing else, only "MOTHER!" for the rest of the night. We made him as comfortable as possible on the carpet; at least he wasn't falling out of things.

During the last round in the morning some of the residents asked, "Who were those children? They sang beautifully."

The day staff came in smiling and happy, to be greeted with two exhausted women, us. We said to the Matron, the night sedation had not worked and that he, Charlie, should be given something stronger, as we could not go through Christmas night with a repeat of this as well as our entire work load. When we left we did admit to each other that our nerves felt slightly rattled. Off we went home to cook Christmas breakfast for our own families and to open a few presents before going for a really earned sleep.

My husband watched me walk up the road, and he

said that I looked unsteady on my feet so he ran down the path to help support me. As I walked through the front door it was to the lovely smell of our turkey cooking. It was prepared and put in the oven on a slow heat to cook all night. We always bought a large one as we would send over two meals for Nan and my Dad for their Christmas dinner.

Christmas night wasn't any better at work. We started the night with a sherry with the Assistant Matron Eunice, a cheerful woman, and had a chat before she went off to the flat. Things appeared quiet for the moment and so after the report we looked in on Charlie. He had been given a strong sedation and looked peaceful. Mary was out for the night locally, with her daughter and family. They would be bringing her back after tea on Boxing Day. Emily's temperature was down and she was feeling much better. Our main problem was a man named Mac, a Scotsman who was normally very pleasant.

He had brought up his five children by himself when his wife had died. He was put into our care because his family were finding it hard to look after him. He seemed to be suffering with a high temperature. There was an almighty crash and again we had to hot foot it upstairs. Where was he? He was stuck in the small toilet just a few yards from his room, mumbling away to himself.

"Mac," we called. He did not respond to us, just kept muttering to himself. His head was fixed in the corner by the opposite side of the door opening. I tried to squeeze in but there wasn't enough room. "It's no good, Christmas night or not, we will have to get the Fire Brigade out. They'll have to take the door off."

We knocked Eunice up and told her that we needed the Fire Brigade to help. "OK," was her reply. They came roaring into the drive and two gorgeous men descended and rang the bell. Eunice rushed forward introducing herself; Pat and I just stood there smiling.

"Let us go and assess the situation now," said Bill. "OK," said Eunice. Really it was 'Step aside, little ladies, we are here now'.

What happened next was horrendous: Bill, the large one, forced the door open with his body. Mac was making loud animal noises as it sounded like his cranium was being crushed. The three of us felt as if we were about to faint, at the thought of what he was doing to poor Mac.

"You fool," I shouted, "we could have done that and we are not as big as you."

"Well, I have the door open, don't I?"

We thought that they would unscrew the door or cut it off. We felt very disappointed with Bill and obviously so did his colleague, Freddie. Instead of offering Christmas drinks, chocolates or cake and a chat we said goodbye as we had to deal with Mac and his crooked shaped head and his large bright red face.

"I thought I was going to die," he said.

I stared at Pat saying, "This is not good!" With ice packs placed on his face and head, and painkillers, he was put back to bed. He settled down into a light sleep. Every quarter of an hour we went to him, to make sure he was all right. Pat and I agreed if we had been in charge we would have sent him to hospital, for proper observation and for an X-ray. We didn't have the last say though and so we had to do the best we could for him throughout the night. It seemed to take a while for his personality to be his old self again: darling Mac, he really was a lovely man. He did not appear to remember any of it, lucky for him. He did make a good recovery though, lasting another four years before he died.

Several months later there was an outbreak of tummy bugs. Let's not delve too deeply, it was awful! With a constant round of cleaning up of residents and bed changing, all that washing, it felt like it would never end. By midnight we were very behind with our duties. We went into the kitchen to discover that we had not locked the back door. It was open and this immediately made us feel nervous and vulnerable.

The next ten to fifteen minutes were taken up with checking all the doors downstairs. Afterwards we decided it was time that we sat down and had a drink. Pat made us a coffee and we were about to take our first sip when we heard the running of footsteps up above us along the corridor. A fire door slamming shut. Armed with walking sticks (I have used these a few times for protection) we climbed the stairs to check all the rooms, the two bathrooms and toilets: nothing. We descended to the lower section of sixteen bedrooms, bathroom, toilets, sluices, sick bay, ironing room and the drying room.

At the very last bedroom along the corridor a sharp gust of wind came underneath the door rattling it. It had come from the emergency exit door within the room. We pushed open the bedroom door, entering the dark room. A timid voice could be heard, "Thank goodness you have come! I was on the commode and this ugly man came bursting in!"

Oh bless, it was Maggie May. "I had such a fright. Who was he?"

"Don't worry, let's get you back to bed. Would you like a hot chocolate to help you get back to sleep?"

"Yes please, nurse."

When we returned to the front hall we noticed that the big bottle which had the charity money in was gone. The staff, residents, family and friends had been collecting for a long time. There was a lot of money in that bottle for a children's charity.

"What a rotter!"

Again we reported this to the Assistant Matron on duty and then went off to make the hot chocolate for Maggie May. A little time passed as we took the opportunity to butter the bread for the morning breakfast, since we were running behind with our duties. As we went into Maggie's room it felt different: ice cold. For a split second I could see a woman who looked something like Maggie and then she disappeared. I placed the cup and saucer on the bedside table and gently whispered Maggie's name. I lifted her small arm to feel for a pulse: nothing. Pat tried and we agreed that she had gone. Laying her flat and in a comfortable position we left to call the Assistant Matron about her death. The Doctor was informed. We sat down together and cried. At least now she is at peace and with loved ones on the other side. She never married and lived most of her life with her mother and sister.

I think it was her Mum I saw, who had come for

her. Maggie was left the full hour for her spirit to depart from her body. When we laid her out, do you know we did not have to touch her lips, for she was smiling beautifully? God bless you, Maggie May, and that was her real name.

It has made me cry after all these years, sitting, thinking about the people who influence your life and who can be recalled in the memory so quickly. People who have come and gone during my life and not just family and friends: our Maggie May.

Every season we put on a show for the residents, their families and friends.

The Matron and her husband, the Superintendent, helped to brighten their residents' lives, which was a wonderful thing to do because they didn't have to bother.

I don't know if anyone can still remember the Tiller Girls from the sixties programme 'Sunday night at the London Palladium'. We started out with six ladies.

The show that was chosen was Snow White. The Matron was a good sport and was in a trio that sang Gilbert and Sullivan's *Three Little Maids from School*.

My dearest friend Elaine, who was by then one of the Assistant Matrons, had put forward her husband to do the comedy act. All did not go too well that evening as he got stage fright and went very silent; all you could hear was "Ted. *Ted.* Come on, it's your turn." Everyone did have a laugh, even if it wasn't at his jokes. The show was going well and it was getting nearer to my performance in a trio. My friend Rosie and I were so nervous that we had started to drink vodka and coke. The other Tiller Girl had never bothered to turn up for any rehearsals, but never mind; she said that she would stay at the back and follow us even though it was supposed to be a line of us.

The superintendent was getting very excited, rushing back and forth, asking us how were we, "Feeling nervous, girls? I can't wait!"

"Mmm," we said. This wasn't helping us at all. His face was getting redder and at one stage he was sweating heavily with all that rushing back and forwards. I guess that it was just too much for him as we were wearing black leotards with black fish net tights, a lacy shawl tied around our small waists and a red feather in our hair with red high heeled shoes. His face was getting redder as if he could not wait to see us three ladies high kicking. I felt some concern as it looked as he might have a heart attack. I don't know how on earth we managed to do our dancing without falling over after all the alcohol we had drunk. It all went well and we got remarks from the old boys, "Girls, good legs, such good legs!" Eddie said to me that I looked beautiful and he liked my legs. They had enjoyed that. Bless them all.

Of all the extraordinary things that happened in that home this was to be one of the strangest. It was a terribly cold winter's night this Wednesday evening; we arrived for night duty just before 9.30pm. It had been snowing for a week or more.

After the day staff had left and we were given the

report there was the one car left out the front of the building, close to the front door. This belonged to Robin, another Assistant Matron, a lovely but very eccentric lady who became a very close friend of mine. After the report and checking the back door near the kitchen we did all the usual duties: getting the drinks trolley ready and collecting the medicines. We entered the first resident's room. It was freezing cold, poor Mrs Hayward. Her bedroom window was open but she was sound asleep. I quietly made my way into the room and was about to go across to close the window when I was distracted by what was on the floor. There was a lot of talcum powder on the floor by the bed. The empty tin lay on the floor beneath her slippers and beside the bedside table. The single bed was always pushed up along the side of the bedroom wall. She was facing us and we could see that she was looking peaceful. Pat came in and we both stood and stared at the floor at the imprints that were in the middle of the talc. I asked Pat, "Can you see what I think that I am seeing?"

"Yes, it looks like a cloven hoof, what do you think? Oh look, Jeanette, it seems to be going towards the window."

Pat pointed to the floor below the window. By now it had stopped snowing outside. We tiptoed to the window and looked out. Outside were the same prints and they went over the roof of the car and seem to disappear. We both felt a bit sick and nervous but there was no denying it; we knew what we had seen. If only our thoughts had been clearer, I could have rang my husband and got him to come down with a camera. Here again, something had been visible to the two of us at the same time.

Another odd thing happened to us a couple of years later in the autumn of 1988. We had sat down for a well earned cup of coffee about 3am when we heard strange noises coming from upstairs on the right side of the building. And so we put down our drinks and ascended the stairs. We pushed open the fire door and went forward and opened the first door to the left; this was Eddie's room, he was a Polish gent who came over in the Second World War, and he suffered with Parkinson's disease. His friends and the Matron were in the process of arranging for him to return to Poland for a few weeks visit to be reunited with his family. This would be his first visit home; his younger sister had been born after he had left to join the army and so they had never met each other. Pat cheerfully used to say to him, "I'll come with you Eddie." But he always said, "No, I want Jeanette to come with me!" as he really liked me, dear Eddie.

He spoke to us and said that he hadn't heard anything. He was cold though, so we wrapped him up nice and cosy and left the room. The next room opposite the fire door was a double room with two single empty beds in it and we thought we would take one of the blankets from there. We crossed the room to look out of the window, from which you could see the entire front of the home, the empty flower beds and the parking area. Elbows on the window sill looking out we both became silent and just stared out of the window. Then the silence became something else and now we became too frightened and stiff to move.

What followed was quite unbelievable even to us. The noise came from down the corridor towards us; it was a loud heavy breathing that a person might make with a deep hoarse sort of rasping sound which then entered our room. This thing we sensed appeared taller in height than us, stopping in the room a few feet behind us. We were frozen to the spot and terrified. Neither of us had the courage to turn and look at what it was. It left the room as it had entered and went off back down the corridor from where it came, disappearing to nothing. The room seemed darker and you could see our own breath in front of us. After a while, we found our courage and left the room to wrap another blanket over Eddie before looking into every room upstairs. All the residents were asleep and seemed peaceful. There had not been any of the usual noises that you might expect in the opening of the fire doors that were further along past the other bedrooms. No noises to indicate that they were being opened. There weren't any footsteps, nothing except this heavy, rasping, breathing. We continued to check the downstairs. The only difference within the home was the temperature had dropped several degrees.

So much is unexplained. It would make a good film!

We had many of these incidents that occurred over the ten years that I worked on night duty at the Home. One such was the incident of the buzzer.

It was for most part a quiet and unassuming night. There weren't any unusually ill residents, or troublesome ones, and so everything appeared to be straightforward and we were on track with all our work up until 2.45 am on this Friday morning.

We had been sitting down for twenty minutes and enjoying our rest with a cup of tea and toast, when the buzzer went. So off we went to see who it was. It was coming from the area where there were just three residents next to the flat where the Assistant Matrons slept. It was a Mrs Simms: a lovely old lady, always greeted you with a smile. Well, when we entered her bedroom it appeared quite normal: warm and with a restful atmosphere. She had her eyes closed and so Pat leaned forward to touch her arm. The buzzer was laying several inches away from her hand and she was fast asleep. The poor woman opened her eyes and seeing Pat's face so close to hers, she screamed out loud! She could have died of fright, and so I went off and made her a cup of sweet tea, as Pat tried to talk to her and reassure her. When we asked her had she pressed the buzzer, did she call for us, she told us no, that she had been asleep for a long time.

We stayed with her for a while and as we were leaving and got to the door the buzzer went off.

We turned to look at her and she said, "I never touched it, I promise you!"

And so we turned it off again and then this happened twice more. We even hid behind the open door; she definitely did not touch it.

It was Elaine, my friend, who was on a night duty sleep-in. In the end we had to get her up out of her sleep. She was good natured about it though. In my mind I was told that they wanted Elaine to turn it off. It sounded again and we said, "You turn it off." So she did and then it all stopped. Nothing more happened that night from Mrs Simms' room.

I cannot explain why, but it was a spirit who only wanted Elaine to get up and turn it off. Perhaps they thought she slept too well? Then Elaine muttered a few choice words and that seemed to be the end of it. Back to bed and off to sleep, her words, "I can sleep on a washing line and get a good night's sleep." Bless her, she really is a super person.

Mrs Simms was settled and so we did another check on the rest of the residents. Then we went back to the kitchen and I did the sliced bread and butter for breakfast and Pat put muslin cloths over the plates and cutlery. We made another hot drink for ourselves and went back to the staff room. After a further twenty minutes we heard what sounded like footsteps, somebody walking and doors slamming.

We said together, "Oh no, what now?" Off we went to the stairs that led off up to the right of the building, convinced it was one or two residents up and about. We worked our way along the corridor checking and looking for anyone that was restless.

Not a soul appeared to be awake, how very odd. We continued across the top of the building and then down the left side and two corridors, past the office, back across the front hall to the staff room: nothing. Well, we sat down again and then it happened again, the same noise, footsteps, slamming of doors. We raced off as fast as we could, hoping that we would catch someone in the act before they could get back into their beds. But there was nothing, absolutely nothing. There weren't any changes in the atmosphere, the temperature was normal. When we returned to the staff room we debated who it could have been.

There were only two men that it could have been, but which one?

Sometimes it is best to think logically before doing anything else. We decided that we would sneak upstairs and wait. We did not have to wait long. Ron came sneaking through the doors and into the Gents toilets, then crept back to his room. Before he could get back into bed we nipped into his room saying, "And what have you been up to Ron?"

Turned out he had made a real mess in the toilets and had used that toilet instead of the one next to him hoping somebody else would be blamed. That solved that mystery!

This next incident also was not a spiritual happening but a real life frightening event.

One night as we were hoovering and polishing two of the sitting rooms, I happened to push open one of the large windows to get some fresh air, and as I turned away to walk towards the hoover something made me look back. There stood a young man staring back at me.

I started shouting out for Pat. She heard and raced into my sitting room. I kept looking straight ahead at this man until he ran off. Pat did not see him, but knew that I was afraid. We both walked forward together and shut the window. I rang the police and then we went to call Eunice who was on duty that night. You always knew that there could be strangers creeping about the grounds, thinking that there were drugs or money, or chancing their luck to rob any of the residents. The police arrived with sniffer dogs, but didn't find anyone. It upset and unnerved us: the sense of vulnerability working in that place at night. After all what could we do if we had locked someone in instead of locking them out and they became violent? I kept on thinking he could have had a knife; he could have cut my arm or just stuck it in me. It made us think and then Pat decided to give up the nights and work on days. I did not want to work there without my dear friend Pat and so I left.

This ended a good chapter in my life. You are not always aware of how good it is until years later when you reflect upon life. Yes, it was very hard work, but such good people worked there that it was fun.

CHAPTER 12

My Soul Mate: Marie

It will be over twenty-five years this coming December that my 'soul mate' died. I was awoken that morning by the phone ringing. I still felt sleepy as I descended the stairs. A chill ran right through my whole being as I lifted the receiver and put it to my ear.

Mickey, her younger brother, spoke, "She has gone Jeanette, passed peacefully away five minutes ago." Quarter to eight on Sunday morning. I can still remember hearing my husband crying upstairs; he knew the same as I did, why the phone rang.

Marie and I shared telepathy; we understood each other's souls. I had a dream that my brother had been killed in Germany. Ed was living and working out there at that time. I felt an intense sense of foreboding as I awoke from the horrible nightmare. I really was quite fraught. The dream was about my brother driving his sports car, and crashing it into a wall. Ed has never owned a sports car. My husband had left for work early as usual and after the children had left for school, around ten o'clock in the morning, I received a call from Marie.

"Hello darling," she said down the phone, then silence.

I repeated twice, "What is the matter?"

"I have had some shocking news. The police have just been round. My brother Desie has been in a car crash. He ran his sports car into a bollard last night, and he died instantly."

I had a guilty feeling of relief knowing it wasn't Ed.

She never got over losing Desie. He was about two and a half years her senior and they were very close emotionally as well as in years. I wished I had had that closeness with mine, but we weren't close. Despite being younger, Marie had always taken care of Desie when they were children and that never ended. I am positive she is still looking after him on the other side the way she did in this life. He was the eldest child, and then came Marie and a few years later Mickey was born. Desie had become very depressed when his marriage had ended, and he did not get to see his two daughters as often as he would have liked.

My daughter loved him; he would sit her on his knee and make up some wonderful stories to tell her. Being Irish they were very imaginative and funny. There we all would be, sitting around listening and laughing: such good memories. Desie drank too much though, and we both believed that it had been his wish to depart from this world.

He had been an Accountant; he was really very clever and such a sweet man. He was visiting his sister when I decided to take my daughter with me up to Berkshire to visit her. We arrived at the train station, and I gave a quick call to the house, "Can anyone collect us?" Ten minutes later Desie arrived in this three wheeler car that he had borrowed. I've never felt so ashamed and humiliated in my life climbing into that thing. I do not care if anyone thinks that I am a snob, some things are just too much to bear! It was a Dell Boy car!

It did not take long for me to realise that that was the least of my worries. The car that we were travelling in was hurtling round bends and my little girl and I were leaning with it as if it was a motor bike. Gripping the dashboard, I calmly said, "Desie, we are not in France." In one swoop he switched from the right side to the left side of the road, and not a word did he utter.

I walked through the back door all dishevelled. The music was playing very loudly, and Marie was standing there with a big smile on her face offering me a glass of wine. "Hello darlings," with hugs, kisses and a twinkle in her eye, "You made it then?" Laughter.

"I suppose you think that was clever," I said.

"I had to be seen in it," she replied, "and I thought so should my best friend."

"You do know Desie was very drunk."

Her dry reply was, "Oh, was he?" So very much like her, all very theatrical!

Over the years when I was with her I would dream or have day visions that alerted me to her dangers and mine. We triggered off many; I believe this was because of sharing a psychic connection.

At one period a few years after her divorce, she

took in another divorced woman lodger, Beryl, who was to become another great friend of hers.

I went for a visit on my own without my children. Her son Matt, who was only nine at the time and is very psychic as well, but does not want the gift, was fast asleep in the small bedroom at the front of the house. Beryl was in the back bedroom and so I shared the double bed with Marie. She had gone off to sleep first, snoring like a trouper. It felt as if I was floating, like when you are just descending into a deeper sleep, when all of a sudden this awful face appeared with a finger pointing right at me. It was an old lined face of a Native American. I tried to call out, but it felt as if the room was lifeless and so very still. So silent and with no sound at all, this vision then became an entity, floating above me, and it began fighting with me. It felt like I was being challenged, that it was trying to take over my body. It was the most terrifying thing I have ever experienced in my life. I managed to release my right arm and swung it outwards, knocking the bedside lamp over. I heard Matt crying in the other bedroom, as the noise had awoken him up and probably frightened him.

Marie sat bolt upright in bed, "It's still here, and it's angry."

Then the stillness shifted and a whirling sound was heard within the room. It went really dark: the colour of black against the black curtained windows.

The air was thick which felt difficult to breath. She shouted out to Matt to stay in his room and said to me, "Don't get out of bed, wait until the thing is gone."

When we got up in the morning I looked at the

curtains and to my surprise the curtains were a pale blue and not black at all. Thinking back it had seemed like a black cave that I was in. I just cannot explain it any other way.

Until this day Matt thinks that he had a bad dream.

Obviously he awoke, hearing his Mum's instructions not to get out of bed and heard our loud nervous voices. This frightened him but fortunately, he never saw or experienced what we had. Thank goodness it never went through to his bedroom.

Apparently these houses were built on and around a place called the Mound, in Bracknell, Berkshire. The story goes that there had been settlers, part of a cult, living underground there. I am not too sure where the Native American came from. Perhaps his long white hair and lined sunburnt face confused me and I just interpreted his appearance that way. He was a nasty spirit and I do not want to see him again.

When I had returned home I relayed this story to my mother-in-law, who lived in our home town of Ashford. She said to me she had had a bad experience herself that same night. She had woken up with a fright, and knocked over her bedside lamp, and she could see a spirit standing at the end of her bed. She went on to say when it had happened: one fifteen in the morning. The exact same time when we had had the awful experience. She said that she got up and put on all the lights in their home, to feel safer. It had clearly unnerved her. My father-in-law was unaware of her distress; he was only bothered that she had turned the lights on and had awoken him.

I knew then I had been in grave danger: it had truly challenged me.

Because of my psychic path, I have been sent a strong spirit guide, Jack, to help me with all these situations that happen to me, to strengthen my courage. It is something that happened and cannot be explained. Scientifically there was not tangible evidence. But there are too many unexplained things happening to more people, and we will have to change our way of thinking in the future. There is more documentation around the world now, proving that there are spirits in the form of our relatives and people that we have known in this world helping us.

Lots of peculiar and strange things happened in that house. Their pet dog was aware of the odd spirits from time to time. Jumping, whining at corners: pets are in tune with the atmosphere of their home.

One night when I was on night duty at the Residential Home in Ashford, I was working with a carer called Maggie. I had a waking vision: my friend was in trouble, I said to Maggie, "Someone is firing a gun at my friend's back bedroom window. A woman has fallen down the stairs and hurt her right ankle, trying to get away."

"Ring her then," she said, "if it will make you feel better."

My friend answered the phone, "God, you were quick!"

It had just happened. She went on to say that Janet and Beryl had been asleep in the back bedroom. Janet had leapt out of bed and fallen down the stairs, hurting her ankle. The rest was how I described it.

Maggie turned to me, "You give me the creeps! But I hope you are around when I need help."

My reply was, "I hope not, as you are always in

trouble and that would be hard work!" We both started laughing, and then we went to answer a resident's bell.

The month of August '92 was Marie's last visit; she had come to stay for a week. Marie had had unexplained pains before in her stomach area. This time it seemed more persistent, but by the end of the week it had eased off. The following months for me were dreadful. I'd feel completely drained of energy. I confided in my psychic artist friend, "Don't think that I am being dramatic, Lynne, but it feels like I'm dying."

I continued feeling poorly until November, and then Marie's daughter, Paula, rang to say her mum was in hospital. After that things got worse, and then one night her dead father came to me, "Jeanette, I am coming for my daughter soon."

From then on I started to get well again. I already knew what was wrong, I told my friend Lynne before I was officially told: it was her liver but it had travelled throughout her body. It wasn't only my husband and I who were devastated: our children were badly affected, especially our daughter, as she thought of her as a second mum. She would have loved Marie going to visit her when she was at University, but it wasn't to be.

When she stayed with us, she would sleep in our son's attic bedroom as he had left home by then. Marie was small in stature, and would race up the stairs and throw herself onto the double bed shouting and squealing, "I'm glad to be here." The way she would dress was outrageous! One day when she arrived she was wearing shiny purple skin-tight leggings and a fluffy jumper, and a black hat with a hideous brooch. It was a Tina Turner look alike, with feather type hair and a black jacket and high boots. The doorbell went and my daughter answered it.

"Get in quick, did anyone see you?" as Lara gripped her by the scruff of the neck and thrust her into the hall. I laughed as usual. Posing for us, she had her wonderful big smile, "What do you think then?"

I was speechless on the topic of her attire. "Oh well, let's have some lunch," I said.

Her favourite was crab sticks, Brie cheese, French stick and wine, lots of wine. She went on to tell us, "This was how I turned up at a posh function." She was a trained nurse and had applied to work at one of the posh public schools up around Berkshire as their nurse. I could just image their faces as she arrived, with full make-up as she continued to describe. "I wore three different shades on my eyes." She did have very beautiful green eyes. We laughed thinking of the vision, but I knew that they would have found her to be an interesting person. She had travelled around the world with her parents when they were a part of the Air Force and she could mix with anybody. You always knew when she arrived anywhere as there was plenty of noise. I could never walk in with her in a dignified manner, forget it!

If we were going out for the evening, she would ring for a taxi and the name she always gave: Lady Bracknell!

One particular day I had woken up feeling unwell, after the family had gone off to work and school. I pottered about doing the daily chores. I suffered with bronchial asthma, and my asthma was bad that day and becoming worse. I thought I would take a bath to try and relax. I became very ill and had trouble getting out of the bath. I kept sending a message telepathically, "Help me, Marie." I managed to get out of the bath and wrapped a towel around me. Then I was stuck unable to move. I could not leave the spot, let alone the bathroom. I opened the window and clung to the bathroom curtain trying to control my breathing. The panic I felt inside kept on rising; if I lost control I could easily die.

Five hours I spent stuck in there struggling to breathe. Eventually, I managed to get down the stairs. The phone rang: it was Marie, she had known something was wrong with me. Afterwards I rang the doctor's surgery. I tried in between my gasping to explain, only to get a silly receptionist telling me to ring later, and saying, "You cannot die from asthma."

Marie rang back. I told her what happened. She lived in Berkshire and I lived in Kent, it was not a case of being round the corner. I had previously given her my Doctor's number as I was very poorly over several years so she phoned the surgery. She went berserk down the phone at the receptionist! The doctor came out straight away and I was sent into hospital.

Telepathy helped me. Everyone can do it; it's a case of keeping trying to communicate that way. That's if you find the right people, of course. Gradually I am losing all the family and friends that I shared this with, but I hope I find more.

I went up to Windsor Hospital to visit with Marie; she was working there at that time for a few months as an agency nurse. Being a private hospital there were sometimes famous patients. Diana Dors was very poorly there and did die. Her husband Alan Lake was with her all the time. Marie dressed me in one of her uniforms and I went around with her visiting all the patients! Diana and Alan were such lovely people, both very attractive and in love. I was lucky to meet them and drank champagne with them. Another patient was a young Arab man having his face reconstructed after an accident from years ago when he was a small boy. It was fantastic what plastic surgeons can do.

I did enjoy my time meeting with such a variety of people.

After Marie had died we used to hear her landing on the attic bed: my daughter would shout out, "Hello, Marie!" Since we moved, I often wondered if the new people could hear the noises coming down from the attic. The loud snoring she would make, truly it was like a thunderstorm! Her high pitched laughter as she bounced on the bed.

When I was very ill, my daughter had a dream.

"You were sitting on a double decker bus, Mummy, with Marie, little Nan, and your Dad. You and Marie looked younger, smiling and waving at me." She continued, "Mummy, I know you would be happy to go over, but please don't go with Marie, stay with us." I felt ashamed: it could be easy just to slip away.

But they are not ready to have me yet, and it wasn't my time. And I don't want to leave my loving family and friends yet. I am not worried about dying and it has felt some times that I could just have gone to sleep and not woken up. When I have had very bad periods of illness, family spirits come and hover.

One time my American Grandad, Franklyn Sterrett Wilder, walked into the bedroom with a sense that he was waiting. My husband, lying next to me, must have sensed something about me that had changed. He shook me quite hard and said, "You are not going anywhere, you can't leave us!" He never saw my Grandad, but I did. Still, something obviously had frightened him for him to have done that.

Being Southern Irish Marie's family did have a funny sense of humour, living their lives in a certain way. Marie would cook us a roast dinner but things always happened in that house, people visiting unexpectedly, for example. So quite often we would sit down at midnight to eat. Matt said that his first wife used to groan at him when he felt hungry late at night but he was used to odd meal times when he was a young boy. He went to work and live in America for a number of years, but has now moved to back to England. Marie would have been so proud of both of her children.

Being a non-smoker myself her smoking sometimes drove me nuts, especially when she accidentally blew smoke into my face and I would moan. She'd grimace, "Get off your high horse." I would gladly have her do that now. One of her great tricks, when she didn't have a mirror, was to look you straight in the face and put her lipstick on. I cannot do it, but my daughter Lara can. Funny the things you remember about a person. That's what being remembered is all about, the good, the bad and the ugly bits.

She and her family were wonderful people and I miss them so much. She loved to introduce me by saying, "This is my best friend and I love her."

I believe that the political information I used to receive pyschically about Ireland came from her.

CHAPTER 13

Introducing more pals: Elaine and Lynne

Elaine Jefferies and I have been friends ever since I was eighteen. We met at Salem's, the training Hospital near Ashford. Elaine is extremely pretty (but she doesn't think so) and on the plump side - always on a diet! Her great love was of parrots and parakeets and she gave us many funny stories over the years.

One day I went round her house for a cup of tea only to find her in the garden hoovering the grass and bushes! What can one say about this bizarre scene? She was wearing parrot earrings, and talking to Percy the parrot with a hoover in her hand in the garden! And she tells me that I am the eccentric one!

She can smell a bargain a mile away. Also she has a marvellous sense of humour and is good fun to be with. But she comes out with such extraordinary comments that our joint friend Lynne and I would always look at each other, "Well I never! Where did that come from?" This one time when her husband with getting on her nerves she commented, "I am taking him down to the coast, sticking him in a wheel chair, and saying 'goodbye and good luck', I'm pushing him over the top of the cliff."

"Isn't that just a bit harsh, Elaine?"

She also likes to tread the boards with an amateur dramatics company at a local village in Westwell, Kent.

I have already spoken about Lynne; she loved to draw and was a good artist. She also loved to smoke, drink, sing and dance - in that order. Great fun and a mind full of useless information like me! Oh, and she had a parrot as well, Wally. Both Elaine and Lynne looked after their birds well, but it's one of the things that I hate: birds in cages.

Lynne always believed in me as a Medium, "You have a great gift, fantastic with Psychometry, the best," she would say. Bless her, even when I had my own doubts, she would encourage me. She called me, 'a vivacious babe with magnificent boobs' and so there you have us: the three witches or the three stooges?!

One Thursday we had a psychic evening out. It was a late summer evening and there was still a little warmth left in air.

We had booked tickets for a psychic supper. It was agreed that I should drive: Lynne could not drive and Elaine is a nervous driver. I told myself 'do be ready on time' as Elaine is a stickler about time and gets fidgety. Lynne was the same as me, hopeless about time. I usually make myself late by starting to clean and put things away: things that have been in a pile for ages! However, at twenty to seven precisely, I picked them up and off we went. I was feeling pretty pleased with myself, and we set off happily with non-stop chattering.

Lynne wore a smart linen trouser suit, Elaine was in a summer blouse and floaty skirt and I wore a bright printed dress. And so we arrived, and we made our entrance. The hall was packed, but we managed to find a table with three seats together. A psychic sat at the head of each table and after we had eaten our supper of fish and chips, they started the readings. We all shifted from one seat to another to take turns to be seated next to the psychic for our individual reading. It seemed to work out well. Everybody enjoyed the evening. I knew who would come through for me. I had asked them to visit, the two spirits, and I felt them and knew that they had been around me all day.

The psychic told me my little Nan and my son Jacob were with me. Good! I wanted to hear from them, especially through another person. Jacob was the child that I lost in a miscarriage between having Luke and Lara; he lets me know when my son Luke is troubled and this is what was said to me, "Luke has been hurt and you should ring him." It was true. I rang the next day, and his girlfriend, who now is his wife, said that he had been mugged but didn't want to worry me. Also, he had been threatened with a knife, but he was safe. At the time they were living in a city that had some really rough areas where knives and guns were used frequently, thank goodness they moved away from there the following year.

Then my little Nan spoke, "My lovely Jeanie." She

told me to look after my health. I suffered with bronchial asthma during my adult life and had to be hospitalised on numerous occasions.

When little Nan was around us at our family home, she would tilt all the pictures on the walls. Different members of the family when seeing it would call out, "Hello Nan." I love knowing she is looking out for us and our dear little lad, Jacob Nicky, in spirit.

The evening finished around ten o'clock and we were a bit hyped up and not ready to go home to sleep. As we always behaved like three naughty school girls we thought of a silly adventure. There is a place just outside of the town with a ruined church and cemetery, next to a very large lake. It is renowned for witches' covens and had the reputation of people having seen spirits on and around the cemetery.

And so there we sat, late at night on our own in the dark. How foolish can you be? Lynne said to Elaine, "I'll give you a fiver if you run around the church and back." Elaine is usually up for a challenge but declined, "Are you off your trolley? Not on your life, I am staying put!" Elaine then said, "We had better be going. People might see us here and would probably be thinking that the two of you are lesbians and I am your mother-in-law." I told you earlier Elaine comes out with these weird sayings.

We both turned at the same time and just stared at her, we both said "Lesbians?" Remember we are Kentish girls and do have good sense of madness. There wasn't anyone to see us and anyway, who in their right mind would think, 'Look - two lesbians and they have their mother-in-law with them on the back seat.'

We all were hooting with laughter as I turned on the ignition and started the car. I had to slam on the brakes as before our very eyes an army platoon of six men marched in front of the bonnet of the car. They were wearing full battle uniforms: packs on their back with camouflage paint on their faces. Quite often the Army will do manoeuvres in these areas of Kent. They appeared in the fog and then just disappeared again through the fog. My side window was open but not a single bit of sound was heard. Why hadn't the boots they wore sounded on the gravelled road? They were all looking straight ahead, no grins or winking of the eye that many would do. We realised that they were spirits and the three of us had seen them together. I asked my guide, Jack, who they were. He told me they were soldiers who fought and died in the Falklands war. I shall never forget the frightened look in their eyes as long as I live, those poor young men.

On that sobering thought we went home feeling quite sad, but we were supposed to be there to see it. I later found out the date was an anniversary connected to the Falkland war. Elaine would tell you that she is not psychic, but even she believes that the three of us were shown these spirit soldiers for a reason.

Everything is shown to us for a reason if you're willing to see, often to make you aware how lucky we all are.

Astral Travelling: it means visiting places in your dreams, or even day dreams. But more than this, it can take you to visit people when you feel upset and need answers to questions.

For instance, I have mentioned my close friend Lynne several times. This is because of the psychic experiences and friendship that we share together.

Her dear husband of twenty-five years became very ill. She came to me to find out what I could see and what the spirits would tell me about him. Her father, in spirit, identified himself through me, to talk with his daughter. He told her she had to be brave and this would go on for quite a while. He said that it was serious and that her husband would undergo a lot of treatment. He told me what was wrong with her husband and that he would die from this. I did not pass this piece of information on. It would soon be explained to them both by the specialist. Then later on she would come and talk with me again in my garden, and then I could help her with some of her anguish.

Going forward a few months, Lynne started to ask me some important questions in dreams. It would always be in the format of her and our joint friend Elaine. If Lynne was on her own then I was just dreaming of her. If Elaine and Lynne were together it was a question that needed an answer, which I was given in the dream. Good, isn't it? You can communicate with anyone all the time this way, so have a go. It can take practice, but especially when you try friends or family, it is not that hard. You need to remember how they are in your dreams, to know the pattern of how they show themselves. Once you know the way they come through to you, it's easy.

This particular afternoon I felt tired and so I went up to our attic bedroom for a rest.

There were two beds at that time in the room. One

was a double bed with a lovely rosewood headboard. It was our son's bed and now he has it in his own home. This was the bed my friend and soul mate Marie would use when she stayed: throwing herself on it, and bouncing up and down like a kid, when she arrived. I always told her off, "Stop doing that!" She never listened and just carried on misbehaving. What could I do?

The other was a single width bed made of pine, with three fitted drawers underneath. My husband had made it for our daughter when she was six and because it was comfy I laid on that one. I climbed upon it and wrapped a knitted square blanket over myself: what we call in this house a nanny's blanket, a comforter.

I had my eyes closed and was feeling cosy and warm, that lovely sensation before you are about to drift off to sleep, when something incredible happened. It felt as if one of our two dogs had jumped up onto the bed and lay along my left side of my body. I still kept my eyes shut. The warmth I could feel felt familiar and did not alarm me at all. I lay there with my eyes closed, still thinking it was one of the pets. All of a sudden, a weight the size of a head rested on my left breast. I opened my eyes and it had gone. Still there on the bed covers was the indentation of a body. I knew it had been Lynne that had visited me.

Twenty minutes after, I got a phone call from Lynne. She told me she had been crying over her husband two nights ago and she visualised herself getting into bed with me, just like I had felt. She was feeling traumatised with what was happening to her beloved husband. Visiting me, she said, was like a child going to their mum for reassurance and love. I was given a lot of comfort from that myself knowing she came to me. It took two days, but her entity made its way and found me.

The psychic world can be so fantastic at times, don't you think?

CHAPTER 14

Guardian Angels: human and spirit

I do believe in guardian angels, both spirit and human. My earthly one is my friend Julie. She has always been everything to me, like a sister. If I had not had her in my life, especially as a child, I would have been very miserable and lonely.

My brother, Ed, was the favourite child. As soon as I was old enough to understand, my Mother informed me, "I don't like females." The next line being, "I never wanted you, I tried my hardest to get rid of you." On and on, like it was a mission from God, Mum bleated, "I sat in a hot bath, took some pills and downed a bottle of gin. And still you clung on in there. I could not get rid of you for love nor money." I looked up at her thinking, "You bet."

I have heard this story over the years and, in fact, so have many complete strangers. We would be having a pleasant time out together, which unfortunately did not happen very often. Then out of the blue, she would inform bewildered people around her of the fact that she did not want me. "This is my daughter," she would say and explain how she tried to get rid of me. I quickly learnt it was best to say nothing. So I always would stand there with a silly smirk on my face. She liked to shock people, and make people feel uncomfortable. No wonder I was born so quickly - I needed to get out of that womb as fast as possible! Apparently I only made small whimpering noises when I was born: obviously hoping to be inconspicuous! It seemed the only thing in my favour. My brother yelled his head off when born. So it's probably the best compliment she bestowed upon me: "You were a quiet and good baby."

Back to Julie. We used to tell everybody that she and I were sisters. At school we told people we had different fathers, and that was why our surnames were not the same. Quite bright for those days, telling fibs seemed to come quite naturally to us, which is a bad thing: especially for a good Catholic girl like me. One of the things we did, like many children do, was to have a club with our neighbouring friends. It was held every night after school, taking turns in each other's sheds. No boys allowed. Being kept out did not please my brother. We would put a piece of cloth over the window so he could not see in. We would also push something heavy up against the door.

"You can join us if you say the password."

"I don't know it, nobody has told me!" he would shout and scream. "Let me in you bitches!"

There would be four or five of us huddled together, giggling and laughing, looking at him through a splintered hole in the door, as he went purple in the face with rage. When we all came out he threatened to get us all and chased us, only it was me he would try to get hold of. Julie would stand between us and then they would fight. Julie's height and build gave her an advantage compared to me as she measured the same as him.

We had some wonderful times, making up stories and acting in plays which were held and performed in my back garden. We girls loved to go roller skating around the streets and up and down our garden path. This path was not particularly long. It went from the front, passing the side gate and back door, which was actually at the side of the house. It continued on past the coal bunker, the outside toilet and the adjoining shed. I must have driven my Mother crazy, as I did this back and forth at least a hundred times a day, trying to pirouette on my skates, such was my joy. I would pretend that I was a famous skater. Julie and I skated right around the housing estate.

Also, we loved to ride our bikes for hours on end to the seaside town of Dymchurch, past the town and cycling along by the sea front.

This was about eighteen miles away from our homes. For lunch we had a couple of sandwiches and an apple in our saddlebags. There was a place called the Ford at Chart Leacon. The river ran from behind the Victoria Park, where it was really deep and continued up through the Ford and then went into a stream. The boys made rafts and we girls would climb upon the rafts and let the boys paddle us up and down the deep river. There was a single path bridge with metal sides above the shallow part of the water and we were able to ride over the path or through the water. Our childhood was care-free and not as restricted as today's children.

We were girlie girls, but dare-devils as well. Julie and I each owned a small plastic umbrella with a pattern of small yellow and green flowers. We would climb up on top of the shed with the corrugated roof, holding our umbrellas up above our heads, and then we just jumped off like cats with nine lives.

Ashford was a town with a lot of history. It has made me so cross how it has been so spoilt, just like many others all over Britain. We would meet up with other girls and boys from the area and go up the woods surrounded by fields to play all day. The farmers didn't complain about this as long as we shut the gates and did not harass the animals. Drinks, sandwiches and sweets were shared between all of us, although the girls provided most of it. It was called the Cuckoo Woods, a fantastic place to have such fun in. It was a thick wooded area with a magnificent tree: the King tree.

The King tree was huge and had lots of nooks and large holes to sit in. One day the boys brought a thick rope and stick for sitting on and hung it from a branch that we could swing out on, over a sheer drop of twenty to thirty feet. We took it in turn to climb on it and be pushed out into the fresh air - praying it would hold the weight and not break! Nobody got hurt, thank goodness.

Poor old Greek Stella was made to go on it first as she weighed the most, being on the heavy side. Her father was the head of the scouts and so that was enough to get her elected to go first and to carry any rucksack that was needed for our trip out for the day, poor Stella. I loved my Stella. She died many years ago now. It was all because her weight had got out of control: she was over twenty-five stone. After both of her parents had died and left her money, she went in for an operation to have a band put in to reduce her stomach size. She died a few days later with complications. I had asked her not to have it done, but she thought it was the answer to her problems. We shared lots of good times and I have many memories of her.

Back to the story, this day my friend Jane made the mistake of bringing her black Labrador dog, Sooty, with us. The cows were grazing in the field next to the woods and we had to go over the stile and through that field. The cows started to gallop in our direction. We all ran as fast as we could as if the Devil himself was after us all. It transpired that heading for the woods trying to hide from cows is not a clever thing to do! In came the herd, mooing: it was the dog that they were after. We were all trying to push and pull the dog up a tree and we all crouched in different places on the tree. Jim, Stella's boyfriend, had the dog in his arms. Unfortunately, the yelling and shouting made the dog panic and it jumped out of Jim's arms and landed on the back of a cow.

"Look," Jim cried, "it's like a rodeo cowboy!"

With screams of laughter and fear, we watched this poor dog sprint off the cow's back and run for its life across the field, followed by the herd of mooing cows. Well, the dog found its way home.

Funny how reluctant it was every time we appeared to take it out for a walk. It never again would go near the lanes heading for the woods. In fact, it had to be pushed out the door to make it go out with Jane again. Her Dad would sound cross, looking at the dog, not knowing the true story. The dog would look sheepish and we children would laugh.

Another pastime in the summer holidays happened when the council sent the men to cut all the grass with the big lawn motor machines. Years ago there were lots of grass areas around the housing estates, and allotments, trees and other places for children to play. Growing up in the fifties and sixties was wonderful. With all the cut grass we would make huge houses and climb inside them, the boys would jump on top of them and then fights would happen. Julie and I loved making Roman walls in the allotments with the grass, 'this is our bathroom, and this is our bedroom.' We would play for hours until dusk.

We could play in the streets as there weren't many cars that came up and down them; just one or two neighbours owned cars. Playing rounders on the green sometimes came to an abrupt end when one of the boys got too enthusiastic with the bat and hit a window with a ball and we quickly dispersed, running off to hide! Naturally we had the Spanish inquisition later from the parents and punishment was dealt out to the criminals!

Julie was my heroine. If Ed hurt me, which was quite often, she was there to take care of me.

I realised quite early on how fortunate it was, not only for Julie but for me as well, that she had such happy parents. They were truly wonderful people, warm and generous. They treated us the same, like I was the younger daughter. They gave us our nicknames, Jab and Jaw, made up from our initials.

The only time I did not appreciate her mum was when she helped my Mum perm my hair, as I was going to be a bridesmaid at Aunty Christine's wedding in a week's time. It took them so long putting in the curlers!

"Have you finished yet?" I cried.

"Oh no!" They were laughing loudly for they had arrived at the back of my hair only to discover that one had rolled the curlers up and the other had rolled them under. That night I could not sleep as the pins holding the curlers in place were sticking in my scalp. The next day when they were taken out disaster had struck! Mum, Dad and Ed stared at me without saying a word. I looked in the mirror. I rushed round to Mrs Bowen, "Look at my hair!" She roared with laughter. It was a mass of tight curls!

"Sorry," she cried, "Never mind," as she tried to comb it.

Julie had different cereals for breakfast than we had and I would look on with big eyes pleading for Joan to say, "Jeanie, would you like a bowl?"

"Yes, please!" I had already eaten. I was not hungry; I just did not want to miss out on eating those delicious cereals with such flavours. My build was slight and I never put on any weight, I was very thin then. For her part, Julie used to love coming to my home, especially when it was to have Sunday lunch: she always said that she loved my Mum's roast potatoes!

Once a week she would have a magazine, called Jacky, delivered by the postman. I felt a little bit envious of her having it. I was not allowed to touch it until she had read right through it first. But it did not matter as she was such a good and generous friend.

Julie's Dad, being artistic and clever with his hands, crafted many things from wood. Just think, we had our very own see-saw in their back garden. Many happy hours we spent on that, up and down, singing and laughing.

One day we heard someone pass wind the other side of the fence, so we started to laugh, saying, "Trump! Trump! Trump!" Mr Bowen, Julie's Dad, flew at us like a madman. He slapped us both round the ears, saying, "I'll not have that kind of talk from you two!" With tears and red ears, we called it a day. Gordon was not normally heavy handed, but rather the reverse. He told us to behave properly as young girls should behave, nicely. Gordon and Joan. I thank God when I think of them and the good times we shared.

Julie's parents were a very special couple, I was devastated when they moved. I was fourteen at the time. I still visited them sometimes. I'd ring the door bell, and stand on the doorstep waiting, with a lettuce, a pot plant and a big smile. The door would open. "Hello, can I stay?"

"Come on in, dear." There would be a big sigh of relief from me. Julie willingly always shared her bed, home and parents with me.

Julie and I have remained good friends to this day accepting each other just as we are, faults and all. We had not seen each other for years as our paths went off in different directions but then they crossed again. Now we seemed to have been guided back together along this path with new adventures to come in the future.

Although we never shared any psychic experiences together, there will always be a great bond between us. I love her, she is a gentle and a sweet person. Her two daughters are my goddaughters, and they are very much like her. I have to say I am lucky as many people seemed to have been sent to help me in my life. That family were next to my dear Nan Wilder in the care and love they gave me.

My Heavenly Angel

I was in my early forties and feeling down hearted, because recently I had lost my dearest friend Marie, my soul mate.

We had had a very powerful psychic connection together. Being psychic I knew that she would always be around me. But it was not going to be enough for me, knowing that I would have all those years to be without her in this world. Not having the hugs, affection and toothy grins we shared is a great loss to me.

In the next world she will be waiting with a bottle of wine, and smoking a cigarette, probably saying, "What's taken you so long?" She tried to live life to the full. She had a smile for everyone, and my children adored her. So her passing was an event of great sadness for us all, not only for me. I realise now that I grieved far too long for her. My therapy was watching over and over again the films *Thelma and Louise*, and *Fried Green Tomatoes at the Whistle Stop Café*. The friendships between the ladies in each film gave me comfort. On this particular day, having heard one of our favourite songs on the radio, I was standing in our lounge sobbing, when something incredible happened.

At first I had a warm sensation go through me, and I could sense something huge rising up behind me. I did not get frightened by this; I just could not believe what was happening. The wing spans had to be six foot either side of me. I felt engulfed by the presence of this Angel, and I asked, "Who are you?" The voice said, "Raphael. Go and look me up." And so the next day I did just that. I went into a book shop and found a book on angels. In the book he wore red and gold, and his hair was a deep reddish brown. This was just as I was shown in my vision. The Archangel Raphael is sent to heal. I felt over the moon at what I had experienced.

A week later my husband and I were invited to a social evening - a husband and wife and a mutual friend. We all had discussed psychic matters openly before and I told them about Raphael. One friend wanted to know more, saying that she believed me about the experience that I had had with the Angel.

I was greatly surprised when, as we were on our way home, my husband told me that the other friend had asked him in the kitchen later that evening if I was having a breakdown. Previously, this friend had said she believed in the spiritual world. I used to give her lots of answers to her questions, and now she was suggesting I was having a breakdown.

"Please don't tell anybody else, I don't like the idea of people laughing at you behind your back," said my husband quietly. He believed me, and I did listen to what he said. I tell only people that I can be sure truly believe as I do.

Ever since the Archangel Raphael appeared to me, my asthma has improved. I do not have asthma attacks any more. I am not affected by the pollen as I was: my allergies seem to have gone, even although living in the country we are surrounded by fields of rape seed. It was not just my asthma which improved but my emotional state too.

I have not seen him since. But I've heard the wings flutter. Then I know who it is around me. I feel myself smile and I know how lucky that I am.

CHAPTER 15

Back to family: my brother and my Daddy

Between the ages of sixteen and eighteen my friend Julie's family were to be my salvation again: they took care of me when I found that I wasn't welcome back in the family home at the weekends.

The thing was that Ed and I were both left bereft after our family fell apart. In those days the shame was terrible. I felt as though everyone was talking about us. I don't suppose they were. It was indicative of how raw my nerves were and how insecure I felt.

My brother Ed was Mum's favourite, so he took it to heart that she just brushed him aside. I'm sure that his behaviour towards me was a direct response to the hurt he must have felt. His emotions at sixteen were all over the place, and so I became his object of dislike. He said he did not want me in the house, and so I had to look around for people, other than family, to help me. For many of my earlier years I hadn't been able to get rid of a sense of rejection. I can say now that it has been years since I have had that emptiness within me.

It was all part of the experience that is called life. I am sure that I became a stronger person because of it.

My brother and I have had many adversities in our lives, but we have picked ourselves up, and moved on forward. Since our Mother died in the year 2010 we have realised that she did not want the two of us to become friends, like a brother and sister should be. She was a compulsive liar and the things she said would ruin reputations. Her family and friends were often unaware of what she was saying. If you don't know what has been said about you then you cannot defend yourself.

Dad never said anything to Ed about his behaviour towards me. Once Mum left Dad went into a depression, which probably never left him throughout his life. It was very hard in trying to get him to the Doctor about any health issues: taking medication was something he did not agree with.

I haven't said anything much about my own Dad yet, as it is sad and distressing to me. But I will say he was very psychic, but afraid of his great gift. He saw many spirits at the New Inn pub when we all stayed there. When Dad and I discussed our gift, he said that he never wanted it. (I got my gifts from him as well as Nan Staveley.) He never wanted me to use my gift; I think that perhaps he felt afraid for me.

Once, I made the mistake of saying about this woman I could see that stood at the end of his bed.

That was it, he packed his bag and more or less moved in with poor little old Nan. It wasn't a good thing for either of them long term. Nan was very particular about everything, and Dad wasn't. They loved each other but got on each other's nerves. In later years he became a bit of hermit.

Since he died I miss him so very much. His handsome face, and his goatee beard, funny rhymes, strange noises and ways. He made this loud noise: the same sound 'Hoo-ah!' as Al Pacino made in *Scent of a Woman*. My Dad was a quiet man, who loved drinking too much.

He was hard of hearing, or maybe had selective hearing. Nan and Dad drove me crazy with their conversations. Nan would repeat the same thing that Dad had just said a minute earlier! When I would arrive home after being in their company, my family and my husband would say, "Why are you shouting? Quieter, please!"

His hearing problem could be a little bit embarrassing at times. We were sitting in the hospital waiting to see a consultant about Dad's lungs. The room was full of people and I was trying to hold a private conversation with him. His daughter-in-law's brother had committed suicide: he had hung himself. Three times I had to repeat this, getting louder and louder and redder in the face. In the end it was public knowledge and created a debate amongst the other people in the Waiting Room about suicide. The nurses glanced at me with a sympathetic look. Looking into his eyes, yes, I could see that there was a glint of amusement there. I am sure he had heard me the first time.

He loved to read all the newspapers and could debate with anyone about politics and many other subjects. He loved the John Wayne films and felt terribly upset when the actor died of cancer. He would never say anything nasty, or run anyone down, unlike Mother who never ever stopped. The only remark he made was to say that our step-father John had acted like his best mate in taking his wife away and then he would laugh.

He never liked making any decisions about his children or wife, which caused one of the rifts between our parents. I know that he is happier in the spirit world with his beloved parents, and his brother Frank.

I do believe Frank tried hard to be Dad's Guardian Angel. My Dad never got over Frank being killed. He told me that the last time Frank came back for a home visit, he knew as soon as he walked into the room that this would be the last visit he would see him alive. When Frank returned to duty he was killed in one of the tanks in North Africa in the Second World War.

Dear Dad is watching over me now, he visits me regularly in my dreams. Dad came to me the night after I had written about this chapter for my book.

I had written 'I wish that Mr and Mrs Bowen had been my parents'. He said, "Don't say that, Jeanie, you are my little girl." He is right, for whatever happened between our Mum and Dad we are their children. Writing this has been a real journey home, I cry every time I read it. I loved my Daddy very much.

I was with him when he died in the Canterbury Hospice. My husband Bob and brother Ed left Dad's side to get a cup of coffee. I leant forward to kiss Dad and I knew he was going. I whispered, "Look to the light Daddy, look to the light, and you will see them coming for you."

I always thought my Grandad would come for his son, as they had been so very close in life. But little Nan had muscled her way in and pushed him aside, saying, "I have come for my boy, Ronnie."

I felt broken hearted and so cross with him for shutting himself away from us all over many years when he became like a hermit and we only saw him for a few hours now and then. He came to us for Christmas before he died and I felt shocked at how ill he looked. I knew he was dying and he stayed with us for a while. That first night I put him on my nebuliser that I used whenever I had had asthma attacks. I used my nebules of Ventolin and rubbed his back for him. I did try and make him comfortable but he wouldn't let me send for a doctor. A few days later I did anyway but I managed to spend a short period with him before he ended up in the Hospice.

When I visited him in the viewing room the day after he died I leant down and kissed his forehead. I kept saying over and over as I sobbed, "You silly fool, Daddy."

I will be so glad to see my Daddy again in the next world.

CHAPTER 16

Jack and the two Jakes

I don't know how my guide Jack has had the patience with me all these years! When he first appeared to me, it was in the shape of a dark vision. It took me a few years to realise Jack was there to help me and who he really is. I did not think to ask him at first. He tells me he has been with me through many lifetimes.

His clothes are inky blue robes and his face, which was once handsome, still is a comfortable face and I love him as he is my protector.

As a Psychic Detective I have been shown some horrendous sights. I thought as a trained nurse, some of my experiences were dreadful, but it still doesn't prepare you.

Over the years it has usually been female victims or children who have come to me. Jack said to me, "If you are to follow this path they want you to walk, then I have to put you through something bad. You have to know how to cope with the misery of what is shown to you."

I said that I would do this as my path was chosen for me.

It was on a Saturday morning; I got up as usual and went down for breakfast. Soon I felt light headed and a little nauseous and had to go to the bathroom to be sick. I was feeling awful and so I crawled back into bed. My daughter said, "You look dreadful Mummy, can I get you anything?"

I said, "Thank you, I think it's a migraine and I'll try and go back to sleep again." About 10am I was shown some ugly images of a young woman being tortured and then murdered. Her wailing and crying continued all day. I told my girl and said, "Do not tell your Dad about what I have said."

By 6pm I was really bad, my breathing became worse and I was very distressed. I realised later that I was taken to her last breath. My husband was extremely worried about me and called the doctor. I was given an injection to help with my breathing. It eased off for a while. Three hours later the doctor came out again and tried to persuade me to go into hospital. My daughter was very scared, "Mummy, I am so frightened for you." At 11pm I meditated in the bathroom, and then it was all over.

My guide came and said, "Why did it take you so long? This could have been over in minutes."

"What did you say?!"

I had been shown and taught a valuable lesson. Just because you are shown these visions and feel their pain as a medium, you don't have to carry it around with you. You learn to get rid of it quickly and move on.

"Well, thank you very much, Jack!" Then he faded away.

Here ended the lesson: knowing how to protect yourself from bad spirits and entities.

I was recently told that it sounds foolish to say your guide has told you things as it is not proven that there are such spirits. So, it cannot be proven - I love him and he has helped me in my lifetime. You either believe or you don't. Until a person has such an experience themselves it is a difficult thing to understand.

I mentioned in an earlier chapter that there have been two other people that have seen Jack. One person was my dearest friend, Lynne, the other my grandson Jake.

My daughter-in-law was staying with me at Bramley Cottage whilst the men had gone to France for a long weekend. Alison was pregnant with her second child: our grandson Tom. Jake was only three at this time.

On the Saturday afternoon we took Jake to Hythe to go on the old small train that starts at Hythe and travels to Dymchurch then through to Dungeness. It travels alongside the sea. It was a great day. Being with Alison and Jake was delightful and I just love train rides.

Alison and I talked endlessly about psychic subjects. She wanted to know more about being able to channel and showed an interest in being able to see or hear spirits. I asked her if she was sure and she said yes.

When Jake had been put to bed in the evening I

asked if a spirit would let us know that they were around us. We were sitting in the lounge talking when we were stopped in our tracks by very loud noises coming from the kitchen. They were very distinctive tapping on the flooring: echoing sounds, like a few small children dancing.

Alison said, "Oh, my goodness!" The next thing that happened was a feeling as if someone ran through me and then her: we both rocked to the left as if we were knocked, as we sat together on the sofa. Then it all disappeared. Absolutely fascinating, this sensation has happened every now and again to me throughout my adult life. For Alison it was completely unexpected, and she felt a little confused and shocked. Afterwards though, she was pleased about sharing something unique with me.

Sunday morning started off quietly until around midday.

Jake was in the hall sitting on the first step of the stairs and we could hear him talking to someone. Alison called Jake to come into the kitchen and offered him a drink of squash.

"Who were you talking with, Jake?" Ali asked him.

"Jacob."

Ali and I look at each other as she then continued to ask him more, "The little boy Jake from play school?"

"No, he's like my Daddy."

'Oh my,' I was thinking, 'here we go.'

"Tall like Daddy?"

"Mmmm."

"Was he on his own?"

"No, Jack as well." Remember he was just over

three and spoke in a baby way.

Alison then asked him, "There was another man with Jacob then?"

Nods of his little blond head.

"Did he have clothes like Jacob?"

Nodding his head again. Alison prompted him asking was the clothing long to the ground, Jake was nodding again. Then I pointed to the colour black on the checked white and black print on the kitchen flooring.

"This colour Jake?"

"Mmmm," he said again.

The two men he saw and spoke with were the spirit of my son Jacob, and my guide Jack.

When Alison first told us she was pregnant, I said it's a boy and he will be very psychic, a Medium. There have been many things that have happened in their own home over the years: children trying to communicate with him and his younger brother. There are so many in my family that have this gift. Jake has learnt that his Nan is a Medium. His Mum does talk about it with him but only when he asks her. I do not say anything but, of course, if he asks me about it later I will discuss it with him. My Nan Staveley wasn't good at explaining to me about having this ability and so made life very scary for me and I don't want my family to feel this way about having a gift.

Some people naturally tap into the gift but others need to train themselves. We all forget to listen and use, but those who are meant to help others in different ways in the world go on to do this. There are completely different sources to connect with. A Medium is a person who can receive messages from spirits that have passed over; others need to use other ways to psychically connect.

The sense that I have the most is when a person or persons close to me are about to leave me. Not just dying, but when something has changed in the relationship and it's finished. Most people know this but I sense small changes sooner. But I also do sense when some people are going to die and not because they are elderly. This I would rather not be told.

Some gifts might be used as tools to do certain jobs. You can train the mind to see into other countries, to see a person standing before you as an entity and ask them for assistance. This is what I do in response for requests to find bad people. I can receive some small but vital piece of information that can be used.

You go to the next world with your personality and if you were a poor communicator when you were alive, why would you be any different after death? It can take a while for spirits to find the right person who will listen to them. Patience is needed to understand but in most cases the information that is given to me seems to be almost immediate, or else there is nothing at all.

Training yourself is all about trying, effort and continued hope.

CHAPTER 17

From the outside looking in: using my gift

I would think most psychic people feel rather like they are on the outside looking in. In any given situation when I am with a group of people I have the feeling of not quite belonging, sometimes a sense that I am invisible. I walk a different path but I am not alone: I am surrounded by spirits wanting to help me or be helped.

I can't understand why most people find it so difficult to receive messages. They are given to me in an instant, often from complete strangers in spirit.

Murdered victims stand before me and I can describe them. If I am lucky they tell me how it has happened and go on to describe the killers. So why don't they give me the names? On rare occasions they do.

We are not given the information to be able to understand the fullness of the after-life. Perhaps this is as well; perhaps such knowledge would be exploited by unethical people in this world.

Sometimes you just have to believe without there being scientific proof. I personally think that how it all works it is simpler than a lot of people want to believe, and that they are blocking off their gifts.

My work as a Psychic Detective started in 1994. I attended an audience with the famous psychic Stephen O'Brien and after the show had finished I was able to sit and chat with him. His advice was to get in touch with the Psychic News and they would give me the name of a Psychic Detective who could help me. And so that is where my connection started.

It's fantastic knowing you have a gift but working for the police in England is frustrating. I have met a handful of police detectives who are open minded, but most of the higher ranks are stubborn. This means that the work is often left uncompleted.

My talent lies in night Dreams, Remote Viewing - which can also be a day vision, Crystal Dowsing and Psychometry - the holding of something.

Remote Viewing or Day Dreams are like watching a small movie, with tiny or huge amounts of information that may or may not be of importance.

I cannot claim to have been a part of any programme relating to learning how to develop the skill to become a Remote Viewer. For me it started naturally, years and years ago. I found that I could sometimes see something, for example, I was on the phone to a stranger and whilst talking with them I could see certain aspects of their home. Once I was talking to a lady and it was as if I were doing a virtual walk from one room to another. I said, "You have a huge pile of ironing to do, and you haven't made your beds yet!" With a nervous laugh she said, "Yes, you are right!" This happened with my Psychic Detective contact too. I could see in his house and, as I could see red as a main colour in their sitting room, said, "Your wife loves the colour red." He said, "Yes, that is her favourite colour." If I am meant to see or know then it is shown to me. Try it. Finding a quiet space on your own with no distractions, sit with pen and paper. Shut your eyes. Now try to clear your mind completely, like in a very deep meditation, losing all thoughts, pictures, colours. It takes time to do this and is fairly hard to do; even now, I don't always succeed. It really depends on the frame of mind that you are in. Once my mind is clear I see only black. Then ask the questions that you need answers to: a year, date, time, descriptions. If you have the ability there, it will happen – with lots of practice! When I open my eyes and look at what I have put on the paper it can be quite amazing. You never know what you are capable of until you try. Good luck my friends.

Psychometry is getting information from holding a person's clothing or an object belonging to them. It can give you a little information or vast amounts of pictures and personal secrets. This can provide information that only the family, police or murderers would know.

There is always a thrill for me in receiving all the messages from spirits: all those people whom I would never normally have met are telling me personal things about themselves, family and friends.

Don't forget the enemies that they had encountered during their life on this earth. Remember that you and your family are vulnerable to certain groups of people who will find you a threat. It can be very scary, so be careful sharing the information. My advice to anyone who is thinking this is the path they have to follow is to go ahead and try, but be aware of whom it is you are dealing with.

I don't always need anything but when looking for bodies I often use my crystal pendulum on maps. Many people have asked for my help over the years to clarify certain information concerning murders and wrong doings.

I have been asked in the past about having a film crew with me, which I declined although I knew it would have made great viewing for the television audience. At the time I felt that it was unethical to do this: it just did not seem the right thing to do.

I have worked for the Police Forces in Kent, and in the Merseyside area.

The first murder case in which I was involved was with the Kent Police: a newborn baby had been found in a lake. The case had been going on for several months with little progress, despite media attention and hard work from the police. And so I offered my assistance, and along came my first contact, a studious Detective Constable. It was a pleasant surprise to me that he was very open minded. He had been in the British Army for a number of years before joining the police force, which gave him a lot more experience.

It was obvious that he understood the information I was able to give him, although it didn't mean much to me. It was a baby girl, which was common knowledge, but I could describe certain features, including the shape of the head and what was found with the baby. That seemed enough to convince him.

Although it is wonderful to be given information, it is often frustrating because it is incomplete. Why don't the spirits go that bit further and give the names of the culprits? In this case they went as far as giving me a girl's name.

He said, "You won't believe it; she is next on my list to interview this afternoon."

Well, we both looked shocked! "No!" I said, so thrilled to have given something useful.

To this day everything that is given to me through channelling makes me feel so amazed.

As the next step I was asked if I would go with him to the scene of the crime. A few days later I got a phone call, asking if it would be convenient for me to go the next day. If so, the Detective would pick me up in an unmarked car on Tuesday morning at 8am precisely. It all sounded a bit like MI5 rather than a local murder.

When we arrived at the scene, I was asked, "Have you ever been here before?" I said I hadn't.

"Alright, then show me where the body was found."

So off I went walking around the lake. When I'm near the correct place I get terrible anxiety: funny sensations go through me like radar and this tells me I am picking up the right place. I pointed to one area, and then we continued to walk round the other side of the lake, and I then showed him another spot. He was able to tell me straight off that the first spot had been where the baby was found, and the second spot was where they thought the baby had been put into the water.

Next, I told him about Psychometry - receiving vibrations and pictures - and that hopefully I would be able to give him more details if I could hold something belonging to the baby. The Detective spoke with his superior officer, and they agreed to allow me to hold what was with the baby. I had to sign papers to say that I handled the evidence, in case it should get to court in the future. This was because by handling it my own DNA would be on it. Two detectives took a DNA sample from me on 9th May 2011.

I believed that the mother of the baby in the lake was around fifteen years old. I felt she could be a traveller, but someone who knew the area. I worked with a close friend of mine who was a psychic artist to draw a picture of the girl. As this girl was not dead, it was my guide who was showing me what she looked like, rather than a spirit standing there in front of me.

The baby was called April because of the month she had been born, and was given a proper burial due to public concern.

About five years later, another police detective arrived at my door, showing me several recent photos of a couple they had photographed at the side of the baby's grave. The woman looked remarkably like an older version of the drawing. She had disappeared again. Until today it is still an unsolved case.

I still feel good about all the information that had been given through me. It is down on record, and that is enough. The mother will turn up again sometime in the future. It was a very sad case for everyone involved. Was it the mother who did it? Perhaps, but in any case people should not rush to judge her as we don't know her state of mind and circumstances.

CHAPTER 18

A famous case: the murders of Lin and Megan Russell

This was a very tragic case concerning a mother and her two daughters. The mother and younger daughter were murdered and the elder daughter was left for dead. Mercifully, she survived and made a full recovery. It became one of the highest profile cases in Britain.

How psychic visions and messages come is unexpected and when it is about a murder it can be very chilling. If I hear about a murder and the spirit of a murdered victim appears or contacts me, I stop watching or reading anything in connection with the case. By doing this I can keep things clear in my mind. Sometimes as soon as a murder hits the headlines I switch off in case a spirit chooses to speak with me; if they don't then I will listen to the news. Not every case is meant for me to be involved with, only the odd few.

I am one of the people who are able to find places

where murder victims have laid, which gives me a photo imprint of what I am seeing there.

The Officer I was to be in contact with was a Detective Constable who was working from the Canterbury Police Station in Kent at that time. People who know of him would agree that he was an open minded, kind and professional detective.

I rang the Station to say what I was seeing with the murders. A Detective said he would like to come and interview me on what I was getting. At that time I was living in a village called Molash, with my husband, daughter and our Jack Russell dog, Annie. The terraced cottage was very small, with a porch which led straight into the very cosy sitting room. The cottage had wooden doors with the old fashioned iron latched handles that rattled when it was windy or they were touched.

The Detective arrived at 2pm on Wednesday afternoon and sat in the armchair. He was very tall, 6 feet 5in, and he made the room seem even smaller. I gave him a cup of tea and then he set about writing down the information I was able to offer the Police.

When I had spoken to him on the phone, he had felt satisfied I was giving him good psychic messages. I knew personal things about the family, had an insight into the home and also was aware of something very specific to the case that was not known to the general public.

I gave him a woman's name that was connected to the Russell family and some information that was not in the public domain. My source was the adult victim, Lin Russell. She had come to me several times to tell me things that were important to her and her family.

These were things that were not known publicly, only to the immediate family and that the Police were aware of.

To make sure I was genuine he asked me to go to the area and identify where the murders had happened. The place in question is Chillenden near Dover in Kent. I had never visited this part of the country before.

I set off from Molash, stopping in Canterbury to collect my friend Ginny who had said she would come with me to keep me company. Then we set off the further ten to fifteen miles to Chillenden.

There were vast fields with woods and many roads and lanes; it could be anywhere. We drove up a country road with some small woods on the left; I turned to Ginny and said, "This is it." I felt the special sensations in my head that then go right through my body: a knowing feeling that we were in the right place.

We got out of the car and I had a good look round. I stood letting my eyes follow from the left to the right around in a half circle. First I saw that there were the two landmarks that I was looking for in opposite directions off in the distance: Lin had told me I would see them and it would help me find the place. The water tower was in one direction and the windmill in another across the fields.

Then I walked down the dirt tracks which led me to the horror spot in which the bodies were found. Something which is quite unusual is the fact that I was never ever shown their pet dog, alive or dead. The vision I had been shown was how they were lying when they had been found. Unfortunately the

Detective would not, or perhaps could not, confirm to me how the bodies had been left: the bodies were moved by the police that were first on the scene. There had been a lot of activity around the three bodies, especially when they discovered that Josie, the elder daughter, was alive.

The Detective told me why he had come to see me in the first place: I had given him the same information as another psychic who was living in Wales. To this day I don't know who the other psychic was.

He came another time to my cottage but I did not do so well. Afterwards my feelings were of letting him, the victims and myself down. I realise though it is how it is meant to be.

I was unable to continue any further with psychic work with the Detective as his superiors would not allow me to hold any clothing belonging to the victims. By doing this I might have come up with more information, but who knows? I believe if you have two psychics who are giving you the same information, which wasn't known publicly, you ought to let them continue. It is worth a try.

The outcome of this case was unsatisfying to me. The police convicted someone for it, but it never sat well within me that he was the one who did it. This is my opinion and I believe others shared my ideas!

Unfortunately, he fitted the profile and the police were convinced that they had got their man. As a psychic detective you don't always get the outcome you hope for or think is right.

Sometimes though, the outcome changes later. In the much publicised case of the Wimbledon victim, Rachel Nickell, I sent off some information through a

Psychic Detective friend who was connected with the Police dealing with this murder. However, both the police and my psychic friend believed they had found the killer, so I thought it wasn't to be me that helped with this case.

Still, I always thought that they had the wrong man in the frame and voiced that opinion to many people. There were similarities, in the build and in a certain look but I saw another man walking behind the innocent man - just like a shadow, only taller.

Rachel communicated with me, showing me what had happened to her. I cried a lot over that poor girl, feeling frustrated at not being given the chance to try and help. When I heard of the murders of Samantha Bisset and her four year old daughter Jazmine I just knew it was the same man. At that time my friend Lynne and I drew a man's face of how I thought he looked. When the police got a confession from the real killer, he matched this picture.

I know that they have caught the right man this time.

CHAPTER 19

Working for the family: private cases

In 1996 I was asked to help a family whose husband, father, father-in-law was in prison for a murder that they were certain he did not do. I was recommended to them by a mutual friend as a Medium who might be able to help.

I had never met them before and I arranged with the daughter-in-law for them to visit me at my house in Ashford. Before they were due to arrive I sat and asked 'Spirit, is there anything that I need to tell them?' so that they could understand that I had tuned into the case.

He had already been arrested and charged and was being held in prison. When they arrived I was able to mention a particular name - Rogers - and they were very surprised by this. Apparently, this had been the surname of the Detective that had been in charge of the case. This was really good as now we could carry on and see what other information I could receive that might be of some help to them.

My next step was to go to their place. I wanted to feel the land next to their bungalow, as I was shown in a vision where the body had been discovered and I wanted to find out if I was right.

We arranged a day for my visit. I hoped that I could tell them more about what might have happened to this poor lady. I turned up mid morning and after we had a short chat I asked them if I could walk in the field ahead of them to see what I could pick up. We went into the field, I started walking and then I stopped, walked on several paces further and turned and came back. I said, "This is the exact spot here." They told me that was correct. When I am near or on top of where a body has been found, something resonates through me like terrible anxiety.

What was disappointing for me was that I was getting plenty of information about the murdered lady but they did not know enough to be able to confirm anything and so I was unable to assist them any further. My Police contact in Ashford had not been given permission to liaise with another County.

The family felt better about what I had received, and so I knew that was all I was supposed to do on this case.

Then there was the case where a lady's brother was accused of murdering his live-in partner. I met this lady for the first time when we were both doing a massage course at the college. After a few sessions we began to talk and she told me that her brother was in prison awaiting trial for this murder. I said not to tell me too much as I would try to help them.

I went to her home and asked her to give me something belonging to her brother. When I held his jumper the woman who had been murdered came forward into the sitting room and stood in front of me. She came as an entity. The air in the room became freezing; the sister of the accused man did not see what I was seeing but she noticed the temperature had dropped and a fuzziness in the atmosphere just a few feet away from me.

The victim in spirit showed me how she had been murdered and gave me lots of relevant information, including a description of the man who did it. Afterwards I asked the lady to take me to the area in which the murder had taken place. I was able to find two spots. One was where the police had found her body and the spirit told me the other was the spot where she had been murdered. I told the police that her body had been moved from the original spot where she was killed. They believed this to be correct.

Afterwards I read the manuscripts on the whole tragedy and discovered that Susan, the victim, had given me accurate and very personal information.

The lady and her brother asked me to go to the court with her. It was quite harrowing. They found him guilty because of his odd behaviour on the day and night of the murder, and also he owned the shot gun used in the murder. But his clothes had not been washed and he was still wearing them when he was taken to the Police Station. The forensics found no blood on his clothes and with the injuries to the victim the blood would have been everywhere nearby the victim. He went to prison for life. If you do not admit your guilt when they review your case during your sentence, then you remain in prison until they feel you have completed the sentence passed. I believe he is still there.

CHAPTER 20

Dowsing on maps: looking for Danny

This case was unusual. I had a phone call from my friend Ginny's brother, Martin.

Martin's work acquaintance, Joe, had been told by others that Martin was interested in psychic matters. He had asked for Martin's help. Martin wasn't able to help but thought that I might be able to.

The problem was that Joe's brother, who had learning difficulties, had gone missing in Spain. Danny lived in a residential home in Kent and two of the staff members had taken four of the residents on holiday abroad. On the first day of the week's holiday one of the staff looking after him had looked away for a few minutes and Danny disappeared. What a nightmare for all concerned!

I agreed to try to help and we arranged to meet at Martin's house around 6pm. When I arrived Martin greeted me and ushered me into their lounge where I met Joe.

"I have to tell you," he said, "I am a sceptic."

"That is OK with me. It's natural that you should have doubts. Let's see what I can pick up."

I had asked if they could bring something of Danny's for me to hold. This is called Psychometry: you hold something belonging to another person and hopefully you are shown pictures from that person. I was given a dark leather jacket with the face of a cowboy on the back. Danny was in his thirties but had the mental age of a five year old. I felt straight away that he was dead, but I did not say this because to do this would take away Joe's hope of finding his brother alive. I did say that I felt the people that were looking after him had been too carefree. The next thing that was said to me from the spirit world was, 'Tell him [Joe] don't forget to take your driving licence with you to Spain.'

Turning to Joe I told him this, and said, "You forgot to do this when you went to America."

It had shocked him and his face drained of colour.

"You are right, but how would you know this?"

How would I know?

"How do you think I know? The spirit is telling me," I laughed.

At home I looked through my world maps for Spain. Inch by inch I went over it with my dowsing pendulum: the crystal pendulum spun fast and furious over the region of Seville. I rang Joe and told him that when they had finished speaking with the Spanish Police they needed to go up into the mountains to Seville where there is a Monastery. There was something important there concerning Danny.

They did this journey, Joe and his sister and their partners. At the monastery they found a poem which they all read. It was about death and saying goodbye. Apparently they all cried as they understood the meaning. They realised that it was a message from Danny and they would never see him alive again.

Two weeks later his body was found.

The residential home had sent out a psychic that they knew to find Danny. The family were upset by that; they would have liked me to have gone to represent them.

I saw he was in the undergrowth surrounded by buildings. He was led off by someone who thought that they could help him, but did not understand that he was a man with a child's mind and just left him. He had curled up and fallen asleep in the warm air and died. So he was found in a place not too far away from where he went missing. I had a real sense that I would have found him sooner rather than later.

As a psychic I know that you are not always called upon to be the one to find people or to be the one that can solve every case. I felt happy at what I had been able to do for Danny, with all the help from spirit. I was able to pass on his special wishes to his beloved family by telling them where to find and read the poem. It was a final goodbye from him to his family. In life he would not have be able to think to say these words and to know what they would have meant. God bless him, darling Danny.

CHAPTER 21

Working with other psychics: terrorism and missing persons

I knew from an early age that I was very different to the people around me. When you are working with like minded people, who share your psychic ability, it can be unbelievably exciting or terrifying. I have shared many experiences with several others.

My main areas of expertise are missing persons and the growing terrorism threat to this world.

In the 1990s I received many messages concerning the IRA bombings. For years I was seeing bad terrorist activity: visions of murders and victims, it felt like I was watching horror movies that could not be switched off. I know this sounds a bit farfetched but it is what was happening to me. The Dreams, Remote Viewing and Day Dreams are like watching a small movie, with tiny or huge amounts of information that may or may not be of importance. At its best I can describe places, buildings and people that can be used to clarify what the authorities would need when they are doing their surveillance.

Unfortunately I had nobody to pass on this information to. I often wondered why me, as I did not feel it was possible that I would be listened to. Eventually I was put in contact with another psychic: the Psychic Detective, whom I'll call Harry.

Together we were able to receive very accurate information which was given to the top intelligence agency in the UK. We did this for four years without meeting one another because of a special unique telepathic bond between us. The transition of a thought, speech, a picture or a moving film is a fantastic thing to be a part of. Understanding another person's thoughts and putting them together with your own is an amazing feeling. When you get a good connection with another psychic, this is what can happen giving wonderful results. Once, when I hadn't heard from him for a long time and had some information for him, I transmitted a mental call to him asking him to contact me. The next morning I had an email from him saying ' Was that you?'.

One of the first things he asked me was, "If you see or hear in spirit from a girl called Helen let me know."

Well, I did. It was as simple as saying, "Helen, if you wish to come and see me, please do."

This young woman appeared clearly before me; I was able to see what she looked like. I contacted my friend Lynne, who was a psychic artist, and I arranged with her to meet. It took an hour between us to get the image of Helen down on paper, and coupled with the things she told me, that gave a positive identification to Harry. He gave me her mother's telephone number and I contacted her with all that Helen had said to me: things that seem simple can mean so much to the bereaved.

This is what I said to her mother: "You don't eat regular meals often, you eat cheese sandwiches."

"Yes, you are right," was her reply.

"Also, who loves pickles?"

"My husband John," she replied, "we bought more today."

Helen had said to me that she had seen her mum put roses either side of her picture in the lounge that very day, and she was able to confirm that was so.

Years later I had another message from Helen: "My Mum is sad that she can see the sun shining and she thinks I cannot. Tell her that I can."

It was the day before they had arranged a service in her honour, to say goodbye to their darling Helen, who has never been found. I have never met her mum, Marie, or travelled to her home but I hope to one day. I always know when Helen is around me when the song *A Whiter Shade of Pale* comes on the radio as I immediately get this haunting feeling that she is with me. This is the song Helen told me to listen out for in connection with her. I had to ask my daughter about the words to it and her close friend Emma wrote it down for me. It made some sense to me then.

Harry and I were able to work together on many situations concerning terrorism and murder, as Harry knew the right people to pass on the information to in the UK and the USA. We only spoke on the telephone but sometimes shared visions. In fact, there were three of us who would receive similar psychic messages; if we all received the same then Harry would pass it on as a positive. In all these years I have never met the other person involved.

Harry would say to me, "Let me know what you get." I would be given quite a lot of information by day visions. Then some I would dream about. If it was important I wasn't able to go back to sleep and would be told in my mind, "Get up, get up!" and then I would go and ring Harry. After I did this I could manage to go back to sleep.

There have been many messages given to me and passed on and it can be frustrating as you are not always given feedback. Some are obvious because it becomes public news.

One night I hadn't long been in bed and was just drifting off when I saw a vision of a bridge, the colour and the post code. A voice then gave me Hammersmith Bridge in London. Then I saw a huge explosion above the bridge, like a green light flashing and flying high in the air. That was it, nothing more.

This was a shared vision and predicted a bomb that had been planted by the IRA on the Hammersmith Bridge. It was found and defused. You cannot get a better result than that.

However, the vision that I had of a man standing with a rocket launcher on his shoulders and aiming it at the MI6 building was not passed on and we all know what happened: it was blasted by the IRA. The year was 2000. Every time an IRA attack was about to happen, I would get a message in my head, "They are on the move." Often, I got nothing else but I would let Harry know.

Having ability is one thing, to be able to pass on good and correct information is another thing. To be given just bits of a story is so frustrating: it's like trying to do a jigsaw with missing pieces. I was shown over and over again the Mosque in London, in the same area as the Canary Wharf. I saw a huge building with all the broken glass in the aftermath of an explosion, but not enough information was given to me to say it will be on this day at exactly this time and it is definitely Canary Wharf.

Getting back to Harry and the night dream visions we shared, some of the things that were being shown to us were about Iraq. Between us we were able to pass on that Saddam Hussein was hiding in a hole and this helped the intelligence agencies to capture him in 2003.

Then in 2010, on 29th October, we successfully identified the printer cartridge bombs that had been loaded onto a cargo plane and they were found and defused.

Harry and I had a brother sister relationship and squabbled every now and then. I drove him mad as he said that I didn't listen to him and he drove me mad also! I haven't spoken with Harry for a long time: our Path has ended now and I have another contact.

In 2003 Harry told me of a small group that needed psychics to offer their gifts to help others and I was happy to join them.

The group was formed in America by a retired law enforcement officer, J. E. 'Kelly' Snyder, with the aim of helping the families of missing persons. It is made up of great psychics, hyper-intuitive individuals, as the site describes them, who try to give assistance and help with the authorities on unsolved murder cases and missing persons. Also more individual families are contacting the group with their requests for help. It is quite shocking, the number of cases of missing persons that are left unsolved every year. Within Find Me there is a small group of psychics called The Special Request Group who get the information first. I am one of this group.

Part of the work I do with the other psychics is to give some kind of closure. Whether it is good or bad news, most people need to know. It is also valuable just knowing that there are people who are willing to listen to their own heartbreak over what has happened, that has so badly affected and changed their own lives forever. I have definitely been affected over the years by such terrible, terrible sadness. We hope to offer some sort of positive guidance in going forward with their future. But still so many people cannot do this. The group is called Find Me and you can read about them on the internet at www.findmegroup.org. We also published a book in the USA in 2007 that was called Find Me. I am one of the authors who relate a story as a Psychic Detective.

CHAPTER 22

A journey into our world: the Soul Searchers

This chapter is dedicated to one of my dearest friends, whom I loved so very much:

> Lynne Helen Sutton,
> died April 2008, aged just 56 years old.

Soul Searchers consisted of two players: Lynne and me. We were been good friends for over thirty years, working on psychic business together on and off.

We shared many similar qualities, a great sense of humour being at the top of the list. In fact, most of our time together was taken up with laughing. Non-stop talking too, with talking over each other a favourite activity. Although we always managed eventually to finish what we had been talking about even if it had started at least five conversations earlier!

Each new case was a wonder to us: we loved the

excitement and the challenge of going in at the deep end. We preferred to know very little about what was happening in a home or property, so as to go and investigate with clear minds. We travelled a lot, going to different locations up and down Britain.

Lynne was a Psychic Artist. Having trained as an artist she was excellent at getting the visions we saw down on paper very quickly. There was something great about what we were able to do when sitting and working together. Quite often we saw visions in front of us at the same time, which is pretty amazing. It was like working as one person. Having done this so many times over the years, it was a normal practice to us.

We were asked to go into many people's worlds, to help them out with their confusing situations. Often we dealt with living souls that had departed from this world and not quite entered anywhere else. We would find out what had happened to these restless souls. Seeing their stories unfold during the eighteen hour period in which we worked could be amazing.

We would ask the clients to leave the property at six in the evening. My first task was to walk around from room to room. This gave me a real sense of which rooms were the troubled ones; I'd sense which held the gateway and the exit for the spirit visitors to enter and depart.

Next, we'd put our church candles in as many rooms as necessary, lighting them at 8pm.

I would carve a message into the individual candles. This is done for messages that I wish to send. I am telling you this, but I am not giving all our secrets away. What we did was special to us, and so it probably won't work for other people. It is a specialised job, and it takes trial and error to find out what to do for the best results. For us the close bond between us allowed us to be able to work at the high level that is needed. We trusted each other completely.

One particular job meant going away for a couple of days. Late morning on the Wednesday we left from the station in Ashford and travelled to London. We then had to go from Charing Cross Station to Victoria Station. When we arrived it was packed, but not thinking we just walked straight onto the platform and stood at the rails. The porter came and was chatting Lynne up whilst she was smoking a cigarette; now she would be told to put it out! I said that I had to go to the Ladies and the porter pointed the way. So I was trotting as fast as I could and not looking where I was going and collided with the then MP David Blunkett, who is blind. Bodyguards, the dog and me, we were in a right flap! I thought that I was going to land on him, and I was giggling and apologising at the same time. When I returned Lynne said, "What was all that noise?"

"It was me," I replied. "I thought I was going to be arrested!"

She and the porter gave me a look and roared with laughter.

I said to the porter that there was a long, angry looking queue of people and the porter smiled and said that we should be back there with them. "Oh goodness!" we both said turning to look again. We had jumped the queue! What should we do? The porter said, "This is the train and when I say 'go' run for your lives and get in one of the last three carriages."

"Go!" he shouted as he opened the gate. We ran; I had borrowed my daughter's small suitcase on wheels and at times the poor thing was flying in the air! We could hear the crowd of people stampeding after us. We managed to secure two seats and as the people got into the carriage, well, if looks could kill! I can truly say that we were not popular!

So we arrived and this nice lady and her partner welcomed us with a cup of tea. Afterwards they went out shopping and when they returned they brought bags and bags of food for us for the night.

I have never seen as much food for one evening as she started unpacking! There was a small cooked chicken, a pizza, sausage rolls, a cold pie, salad, prawns, avocado, crisps, a Black Forest Gateau and a Victoria sponge. I swear to God this is all true!

Oh, my! Anyway, when they had gone we settled and started our job - and did not have a bite to eat until eight pm! Throughout the night a number of different things can happen. Usually when spirits enter a room there are cold spots. This didn't happen in our cases. We found the atmosphere totally changed, as if the room became heavy and a bit cloudy. Usually there are noises and these can be quite scary. Each time we experienced some sort of contact, pinching, grabbing or pushing, to name but a few. But it was not meant to hurt us, only to get our attention.

This evening I was pushed by an old lady in spirit. It transpired we were there to find out the story of what happened between her husband and son. She felt desperate to get someone to know what had happened and to make sure that her husband had been rescued by her beloved son. They had quarrelled and the father was so angry with his son that he attacked him, pushing him aside roughly. The son then fell and hit his head and died. The father was full of remorse and was still remorseful when he himself died. Due to this, the father had not passed over and was still in the house. The son also could not rest until he could take his parents over to the other side. The poor mother said that she could not rest until she knew that her family had been reunited and taken over together. And so they were all stuck. The son came for his dad between 1 and 2am. After that the house atmosphere eventually cleared except for the lounge. The remaining spirit was the mother; her son came back for her at 4am and as she now was willing to go on with the son peace then descended over the house.

There is a lot of work to do after the house is clear of unwelcome guests and so we set about clearing, cleaning and healing the house. We also always sent absent healing to our clients before they returned home - not forgetting any pets.

On their return these particular clients asked us what had happened between 10.45pm and 11pm.

They had been involved in an unexpected experience: a loud thunder clap over the building they were staying in. They were in a flat an hour away from us. The landlord of the flat happened to live down the road from them. The noise was so loud that it had prompted him to leave his house to find out if there was any damage to the block of flats, and so he knocked on their door. They had thought perhaps there was some structural movement. But everything looked fine.

At that same time in the evening an ear splitting noise had been recorded on our tape. This was when we were trying to persuade the son in spirit to come and talk with us. He was not in the mood for talking at that point in time and hence the outburst of noise at the house and above the flats.

Later on, he decided he wished to communicate with us. What he had said was that he had been homosexual and his father had very strong views about this: his father had been outraged and that was why he had lashed out at his son. Every one of them had paid the price.

With the night and our work completed, we talked with our clients and then went for a well earned breakfast and sleep.

Another job finished.

The clients rang a few weeks later to say that it was all peaceful and to thank us again for going.

Unfortunately, there are many sceptics who would argue about what I have told you. I have my own belief in what I do, and I believe I was doing something worthwhile.

If you really want to help people find solace in their own homes, you really do have to believe it's for the good and that is why you are there. There cannot be half measures in this line of work; you have to truly want to be there.

I have given up this line of work now; I don't want to do it without my Lynne.

There are many people in homes out there that are haunted. Most of the time it happens to be spirits that have died and have not been able to pass over into the next world. It can get eerie and you have to have strong nerves and a strong voice for this. Sometimes it is a case of be gone, get out………or please go. But the work is not all doom and gloom, it can bring a lot of fun and laughter too.

I would strongly advise that two people do this line of work together. It is essential that you trust the person you are working with. If you are not sure don't do it!

This next case was very interesting. We were contacted by a friend of a gentleman in Scotland. He was a widower and lived alone.

He was in sound mind; again, remember some people are not. Other members of the family had witnessed some of the goings on in the house. There had been unexplained noises in the kitchen when nobody was in there. There had been several instances of different footsteps walking down the hall away from the lounge area. In his bedroom at night there were flying objects. It was making him poorly. He had lost several stones in weight and so his family agreed that we should be called in.

Rita, his friend who originally contacted us, arranged everything.

She met us at the airport. Lynne recognized her immediately. They had spoken several times on the phone. She took us to the Bed and Breakfast where we were staying for the night in Inverness, before going to Henry's home in Aberfeldy the following morning.

What a lovely lady she was! She took us back to her bungalow for tea. Again, this was to be quite comical situation. She was suffering with sore feet and other problems and so she had to leave us to go and collect her prescription from the Doctor's surgery.

Before she left, she set about getting all this food out, and placing it on the kitchen table. Rita was not a tidy person, and there was about a square foot on the table to put all the food on.

"I bought a cooked roast cold chicken to have with a salad," she announced to us.

"Lovely," we replied.

"I have to go and get my prescription and I won't be long".

After she had left we went through into the kitchen and out into the small garden at the rear of the house. Lynne was walking in front of me and she brushed up against the chicken that had been left precariously balanced on top of an assortment of salad cartons. The chicken flew off the top and hurtled out the back door landing on the dirt patch of garden. The cat got there first, sniffing and a lick or two! Oh, no! We picked it up and took it back into the kitchen. Looking at each other, we decided to wash and dry it. So this is what we did and then replaced it in the same position, balancing it in the way it had been left, to make sure Rita would not notice that we had touched it.

It was a struggle to swallow that cold cooked chicken, Rita tucked in and obviously enjoyed it!

When we arrived at Henry's property we followed our usual routine of introducing ourselves and then walking all over the property to assess it for the first time. After, we asked everyone to leave until 11am the following morning.

This gives us the time to do what is necessary in clearing the home. Every home has a gateway and an exit for the spirits to come and leave. This is when I used my amber necklace, walking from room to room. It spun like mad in the main bedroom: this was the exit to the world beyond. The kitchen was the entrance.

We set about laying out our experiments.

On Henry's bed we placed a clean white piece of paper with a coin placed on it. You draw round the coin, so you can check its progress during the night, to see if it has moved.

In the kitchen, that was the entrance in the house, we sprinkled powder on the floor and this was to see any marks that appeared during an eighteen hour watch. If nothing happens between the times you set up to work, then it's not going to work.

We always took four to six church candles which we always lit at eight o'clock in the evening; these have to burn all night long. I was the one who etched a message into each candle. It must burn itself out. This is so the message has gone and the light is there; candle magic has been used for centuries. Again, be careful what you wish for, if it's not pure thoughts, it will come back…………..

Plus don't forget holy water. As a Catholic I believe in it for the cleansing of the rooms.

The spirit who came through to us had belonged to a clan that had lived in the area and that afterwards was traced back to Henry's wife's family. He called himself Benedict. We think he was referring to the Benedictine monks that had lived in the mountains.

We were able to describe him and what he was wearing. My colleague was a psychic artist, and could draw him. He was very distressed, smelly and spiteful. He pushed me during the night and gripped my colleague Lynne tightly around the waist, hurting her. By time it had all finished we felt tired and a bit giggly.

I made a tape to give the family of what had happened during the night. Six in the morning I was prattling into the dictaphone. Afterwards, I rewound it. Oh my, to hear your own voice is a shock as we all imagine that we sound different!

Laughing her head off, Lynne said, "Did you hear what you said?"

"What do you mean?"

"Just listen."

Instead of saying 'the gateway', I had said 'the gate-hole'. It sounded dreadful, but at this stage I was past caring. I was so tired, that was that. We could not stop our laughter, fortunately for us we could laugh at everything. The happiness laughter brings always lifts the atmosphere.

The outcome was a good one. The next day on Henry's return they felt the difference as soon as they walked through the patio doors. They asked us to stay another night and we agreed.

When we had retired to the spare room for the night we had some scary experiences ourselves.

As Lynne was doing a drawing of Henry's late wife, to leave as a small gift from her, she began to stare at me. We were both lying on twin beds; I was lying on my side chatting to her.

"What's the matter?" I said.

"Oh, my God! Your face has disappeared and

another one is looking back at me!"

"No," I said, "Stop messing about!"

I did feel a funny tingle over my face, and then it disappeared. The colour in her face had gone; she was as white as a sheet.

Then we both experienced the same vision: a group of men in black robes, bent right over with the rain, coming down the mountains. They were coming for the man to take him over. That had been the trouble all those years, none of his clan would come. He had done something terrible: he had killed one of his own, which was the worst sin of all. There was a loud bang outside the door. That scared us. I leapt from my bed onto Lynne's with my back against the wall.

We looked at each other and both of us said "Great protectors we turned out to be!"

Laughing, we snuggled under the covers and went to sleep.

The next morning we got up and Lynne cooked all of us smoked kippers. After breakfast we asked rather gingerly, "Did you hear all that noise around midnight?"

"No," was their reply, "we slept soundly."

"Good, good." That was that then, just the two of us had heard it.

They had come to take him over properly: the monks, all ten of them. How wonderful! A week later, a friend of Rita's asked their friend to look up the history about where Henry was living. And surprise, surprise, lots of what we had given them was down on paper as being true.

The spirits were out in force in helping dear Henry. Now, he is even thinking of re-marrying again!

CHAPTER 23

The search for Keith Bennett: unfinished business

Over a long period Keith's spirit appeared to me in a vision in my mind. He showed himself as the public photo that has been shown over the years from when he was kidnapped and murdered in 1963, which is how I recognised him. All he ever said was, "Come and find me, Jeanette." Then I would not see him again for a while, sometimes for years. It is well known that he has gone to many psychic people but I always felt he wanted me to go to Saddleworth Moor and look for his grave.

In 2010 I was driving my car towards where my husband was working on a friend's house and I had the radio on. In France where I live they have a Radio Station called Nostalgie, it plays 60s music. I was listening to this and where the radio shows the name of the station it flashed my name Jeanette, then it went and flashed again Jeanette. It was spelt how my name is spelt: there are several ways of spelling it. I mentioned it to my husband as it was a bit weird.

When I got home I sat on my bed and I asked, "Is that you Keith?" Then I was shown his face. He said again, "Come and find me, Jeanette," then he said that he was buried beneath a large jutting out rock that was in the higher earth above him and near water. I rang and spoke with my daughter-in-law Alison about what had happened and said that I had made up my mind to go. As I was talking with her on the phone, my whole body lurched forward as he ran right through me. He was an excited boy and it had rocked my body back and forth quite violently.

I rang my daughter and she agreed to take a few holiday days that she was owed and come with me. My husband and I were going to the wedding of a friend's son that was taking place in the city of Le Mans in France. The happy couple live in Jersey and were coming to France for their wedding as the bride is French. They had booked a minibus for themselves and family members. I asked if I could return with them on the Monday morning to England and they agreed.

I booked a stay in a Bed and Breakfast for three nights in Uppermill, near the moors. My daughter had booked a rental car for us to go in because her car had a few problems. As it turned out the car gears in the hire car were not that good and driving all the way up country near to Manchester and back was really bad! But on the positive side it turned out to be a wonderful time shared with Lara, great fun as well as doing a professional job.

This is Lara's accounts of these few days from May

2nd. I have deleted the names of the people I contacted and also the coordinates of the spot I located. Before going I did not know many details of where the other bodies had been found as it would cloud my judgement. This is how my mind and body works on finding where bodies have been.

Notes.

Wednesday 2nd June 2010
Travelled along the A635 through Saddleworth Moor, on our way to Uppermill.
We drove very slowly so Mum could take in the vast moors. At one point looking down into the valley Mum started to feel high levels of anxiety.
Looking down to our left we could see Dove Stone Reservoir which Mum felt was important and would want to go and take a closer look at. As we went further I looked for roads that would take us closer to the reservoir for the next day.

Thursday 3rd June 2010
The first thing we did before going to the moors was to buy an Ordnance Survey map as neither of us had been to this part of the country before.
Drove back along A635 and Mum once again felt anxious. Marked on map as point (1)
We travelled further along the road and at point (5) which I later marked on the map felt she should pull over.
She got out of the car to get a feel for the area. Turning the car around we travelled back to an off the road parking area, point (2) which had walks. This area had long walks heading down for miles which would take us to the reservoir. Mum was picking up feelings here. Mum then climbed over a broken fence

as she felt she should and found a viewpoint that overlooked the whole area. Mum felt the anxiety again which affected her stomach. A very strong reaction to this area. Mum started to walk down ahead of me to a steep incline and met a couple that told us that there was another parking area a lot closer to the reservoir and with less climbing.

Back in the car we left the main road and continued to Dove Stone parking.

We parked the car in the car park, and then started walking up towards the Life for a Life Memorial area. Inside we sat on the bench and looked out towards the reservoir. Marked point (3) on the map.

Mum was told that Keith was near water and the south west, with a large jagged rock above him.

She was a little unsure what was meant, south west of where?

We looked at the Ordnance Survey map and I pointed out that we were south west of where Mum had originally said at point (1) on the map.

Mum used her pendant over the map asking Keith where he wanted us to go. It spun over the Weir.

It was difficult to get to, rocky and a boggy area, lots of families picnicking.

We kept a low profile so as not to disturb anyone and on the other side of the Weir Mum walked with her pendant all around the area. She called to me "look" the pendant was spinning so violently it was horizontal, point (4)

I then used the Tom Tom to get the co-ordinates of the spot..........

We both looked up and there was the jagged rock protruding out of the higher land above us.

Later we read that the reservoir was not made when the murders happened, and the spot that Mum believed he is, was where a car or van could have got near to, all those years ago and not been seen.

We felt that this was enough for the day and returned to Uppermill.

After several hours on the moors what my Mum had set out to do was done.

Nobody knew us and why we were there. When asked we just said we are here for a break together.

We tried to be considerate about the people's feelings, as it still must be upsetting for those people who have always lived there.

We went for a drink and some local men talked to us about the cotton mills that used to be around, and then one of the men suddenly changed the subject to tell me that the bodies of the children killed by the Moors Murderers were brought to the mortuary in Uppermill after they had been found. The mortuary had since been knocked down and a car park built. Very interesting, but we still said nothing on the subject.

Previously, before leaving France to come to England, Mum rang the number of the Keith Bennett site to see if we could have a contact for when we arrived. She spoke with a younger man and he said that he would be pleased to meet with her on our visit.

At the Bed and Breakfast Mum called this contact. No answer and so called the Press Officer. He was very abrupt and rude and said that he did not want to speak with her and put the phone down.

Mum tried the contact again and this time arranged to meet him on the Friday 4th

Friday 4th June
I received a Text message 7.42 am.
" Wot time cud we meet at Welli Hole today? The earlier the better" It was the Press Officer.

I replied at 8.15am:

"Hello this is Jeanette's daughter Lara. I haven't woken her yet. We are meeting a contact at 11am."

No reply so I sent "Did you want to meet before or after our meeting with our contact? Can Mum call you back to discuss it?"

No reply, so Mum called him and he sent a text saying the message was not meant for her and he wasn't interested in meeting her.

Met up with contact at 11am a very excitable person but pleasant. Mum told him that we did our work yesterday, but would not tell him anything until after he had shown us the relevant places concerning to the cases.

Mum asked him to take us up to the moor and to show us where the bodies were found, as Mum did not know. He took us up the A635 again. Pointed out Baggart Stones which Ian Brady was photographed, apparently he liked to practise shooting there. I realised that was point (1) which I had marked on the map, where Mum had first had felt anxious but we had not noticed the rocks as we were looking to our left down at the reservoir. We travelled further along and our contact pointed out the area where the recovered bodies were found and that the police had dug and checked. Again this is an area we stopped at point (5)

He then took us to the first parking area we had stopped at the day before point (2) and said that he wanted to show my Mum something and walked her to and climbed the fence to the very spot she had stood on the day before and to look out over the whole area. This was already marked on the map by me.

We then said we wanted to show him what we did on the Thursday, and so we took him to Dove Reservoir, showing him where we went. I took him to the spot Mum had pinpointed and had left a stick as a marker. We both took photographs of the area and he said it fit with the profile of what Ian Brady liked: water, boggy ground, a tree and unusual shaped rocks.

After this Mum said she wanted to help with the search for other bodies that could be buried on the moors. Because we had little time left Mum needed to have the contact's help. The contact directed us back on to A635 which leads to Meltham Moor. At Mum's request he said nothing as she needed to see what she could pick up herself. Mum felt she needed to stop and so we did in a lay-by by Cock Crowing Rock Stone.

The contact said that another lady he took to the area also wanted to stop there. Mum pinpointed three spots which we photographed and recorded for future reference.

I think that after all the time and effort that the police had put in to this case over the years one last effort could be made to rule it out, or have a positive ending.

L

I sent these notes with a letter to the Chief of Manchester Police. In the letter, I introduced myself and gave some references that he could check in the UK and the USA, including a contact for the Find Me group. In conclusion I wrote,

"I hope you will take action on this information that I give you. All it would take is two officers to spend the day there and seeing that it has cost the force years of expense I think it's worth the trouble for Winnie Johnson's family, don't you? I would donate the money if I had it, I help people for nothing. This all could be done now in private so as not to upset her family."

The letter was ignored. I can understand that the Police have been inundated with psychics over the 40 odd years since Keith went missing and do not have the resources to continue with any more searches. I do feel disappointed as I wanted to see it through to the end before Keith's mother died. I never asked for money or any publicity, just to work for Keith.

CHAPTER 24

Here and now: closing thoughts

All of this has led me to where I am now. I have suffered great sadness over my parents whom I loved dearly: my Mum, in particular caused me a lot of sorrow. Now, I will say that I feel a sense of happiness, although still not completely. The past is difficult to discard.

We all try to make the best of what we have in our life and to be content; to discover within one's soul that you cannot always change how other people are or to try and take the blame for how they have behaved in life.

You need to give up thinking you might have been able to change the final outcome. This is what I have had to learn, this is what has taken me so long to discover: we cannot as it is not in our control to do this.

I have shared many things in my book with you, but not everything, and do hope that I have given you some insight into how my life has evolved over the years, especially all the people that have come and gone. I truly hope I have brought them alive on paper so you can join in the shared delight with me.

My psychic path has opened up many experiences for me, the good as well as some bad. Helping others with my gift has been the best thing ever in my life - after my marriage, my two children, their spouses Simon and Alison, and my three grandsons.

My husband and I have been blessed in many ways and also endured hardship. We have had two dogs and three cats, and we valued the love and loyalty that they showed us, especially in the years when I was so ill. My two dogs, Joe and Annie, tolerated the changes of temperature as they knew when the spirits entered the room. They knew when things changed within my body when I could just have faded and died. There have been quite a few times when I struggled to breathe and not to give in. My Joey always kept by me, knowing that I was very ill.

Love to you all, and thank you from deep within me for picking my book to read. I hope you have laughed as much as I have when recalling the funny stories about family and friends.

I must not finish without mentioning my dear Jack who has helped me throughout my life when loneliness has overwhelmed me: a knowing and a big sigh together.

Jeanette Ann Healey